18.95

Modern Methods
for
COBOL Programmers

John Pugh
School of Computer Science
Carleton University, Ottawa, Canada

and

Doug Bell
Department of Computer Studies
Sheffield City Polytechnic, England

Prentice/Hall International

*Englewood Cliffs, New Jersey London New Delhi Rio de Janeiro
Singapore Sydney Tokyo Toronto Wellington*

Library of Congress Cataloging in Publication Data

Pugh, John R., 1950–
  Modern methods for COBOL programmers.
  Includes bibliographies and index.
  1. COBOL (computer program language).
  I. Bell, Doug H., 1944–   . II. Title.
QA76.73.C25P83 1983   001.64'24   82-22978
ISBN 0-13-595215-8

British Library Cataloguing in Publication Data

Pugh, John R.
Modern methods for COBOL programmers.
  1. COBOL (computer programming language).
  I. Title. II. Bell, Doug H.
001.   64'24   QA76.73.C25
ISBN 0-13-595215 8

ISBN 0-13-595215 8

Prentice-Hall International, Inc., *London*
Prentice-Hall of Australia Pty, Ltd., *Sydney*
Prentice-Hall Canada, Inc., *Toronto*
Prentice-Hall of India Private Ltd., *New Dehli*
Prentice-Hall of Japan, Inc., *Tokyo*
Prentice-Hall of Southeast Asia Pte., Ltd., *Singapore*
Prentice-Hall Inc., *Englewood Cliffs, New Jersey*
Prentice-Hall do Brasil Ltda., *Rio de Janeiro*
Whitehall Books Ltd., *Wellington, New Zealand*

Printed in the United States of America

10 9 8 7 6 5 4 3 2 1

CONTENTS

72589

PREFACE

The last decade has seen the production of software emerge as a major problem for the data processing industry. Less expensive but more powerful computer hardware has made feasible projects which would not have been contemplated only a few years ago. Many of these projects, however, will either not be implemented or be delayed due to the spiralling costs both of maintaining current software and of developing new software. Missed deadlines, cost overruns, shortages of qualified personnel, and badly designed systems are familiar problems in what has come to be termed the 'software crisis'.

The need for new tools and techniques in software development has been apparent for some years. Many organizations, groups and individual researchers have attacked the software problem, resulting in an overwhelming number of improved programming practices being suggested. Many of these practices are no longer in their infancy, they have been tried and tested on major projects from a wide variety of application areas. Some have proved very successful; but despite the demonstrated benefits of these new programming ideas they are still generally unknown or misunderstood.

This textbook is aimed at the practicing business application programmer. It discusses proven programming tools and techniques and shows how they can be applied to the development of commercial data processing systems. An objective is to present this material from the viewpoint of the applications programmer wishing to upgrade his or her knowledge of modern programming practices, although the text will also be of interest to systems analysts and managers. COBOL is used throughout this text as it remains the most extensively used business application programming language.

This book is not an introduction to programming in COBOL: it is aimed primarily at readers who have a working knowledge of COBOL but who may not have a thorough grounding in the fundamentals of program design. It is only in recent years that educational institutions have begun to emphasize this important topic. The text is also suitable for a second-level undergraduate course which provides an introduction to business data processing using COBOL. These students should be fluent in a high level language other than COBOL and have access to a COBOL language reference manual.

Several chapters are devoted to case studies, where solutions to typical data processing problems are developed using techniques introduced in earlier chapters. We intentionally do not present nicely packaged textbook solutions. It is important for the reader to fully understand how and why a particular solution developed and why other potential solutions were discarded.

Chapter 1 describes the problems involved in developing and maintaining software and presents an overview of the programming practices followed in dealing with these problems.

Early chapters concentrate on the development of an organized and disciplined approach to the difficult task of program design. Chapter 2 introduces the basic components of a design methodology which is referred to throughout the text as top-down stepwise refinement. This is closely aligned with, although not restricted by, the functional decomposition approach to program design. The text may thus be considered an alternative to texts concentrating on the data structure or data flow approaches. Chapter 3 applies the methodology to the design of a multi-level report program. Additional guidelines for successful program design are presented in Chapter 4 before the design of two classical data processing problems are considered in Chapters 5 and 6.

Chapter 7 describes a subset of COBOL which may be used to produce clear, maintainable and reliable COBOL programs. This chapter is chiefly aimed at programmers with little or no knowledge of COBOL. Chapter 8 describes how COBOL may be used to implement program designs developed in line with the methodology presented in earlier chapters. Further guidelines for programming in COBOL are given in Chapter 9; this chapter also includes the full COBOL texts for the case study designs developed earlier. The current standard version of COBOL, as adopted by the American National Standards Institute (ANSI) in 1974, is used throughout the text.

Chapter 10 describes a top-down approach to the implementation and testing of program systems. This technique is applied to the development of an on-line update program in Chapter 11.

The final two chapters deal with practices which are increasingly being introduced by managers to organize and control software projects. Chapter 12 discusses structured walkthroughs, a method of reviewing the progress of a project at various stages. Chapter 13 deals with the operation of programmer teams.

Exercises and further reading lists are provided at the end of many of the chapters. Some of the exercises raise problems which will be discussed later in the text.

We thank people at Carleton University and Sheffield City Polytechnic for their help, particularly Linda Guay, Mike Hollingsworth, Linda Latham, Mark Shackleton and Neil Willis. In preparing this book we used the facilities provided by the computer centers at Carleton University and Sheffield City Polytechnic: we appreciate the help given by people in those centers. Giles Wright of Prentice-Hall is thanked for his support and encouragement.

The ideas discussed in this book are the result of the efforts of many dedicated computer professionals and we would like to acknowledge their work.

COBOL is an industry language and is not the property of any company or group of companies, or of any organzation or group of organizations.

No warranty, expressed or implied, is made by any contributor or by the CODASYL Programming Language Committee as to the accuracy and functioning of the programming system and language. Moreover, no responsibility is assumed by any contributor, or by the committee, in connection therewith.

1

Introduction

1.1 OVERVIEW

The term "Software Crisis" is familiar to everyone involved in data processing today. In recent years the cost of computing power has plummeted dramatically. During the same period the cost of producing software has continued to rise at such an alarming rate that it is not uncommon for software costs to account for 75% or more of the costs of a new computer system. Software costs in the US are now measured in tens of billions of dollars each year. The rapid advances in hardware technology have significantly increased the scale of projects which are now being tackled and have tended to nullify any improvements gained from recent developments in software technology. These are very disturbing trends which unfortunately seem likely to continue for the foreseeable future.

Though progress has been slow, significant advances have been made in the development of tools and techniques to improve the process of producing software. These developments have covered all elements of the Software Life Cycle but in this text we concentrate on those areas which have most impact on the practicing business application programmer, namely, software design, coding and documentation, operation and maintenance, and the management of software projects. Despite the fact that the techniques discussed in this text are no longer in their infancy and that many proven benefits have accrued from their use, they have not been universally adopted and widespread ignorance and misunderstanding of the methods still exists.

Some confusion is easily understood as in recent years programmers have been overwhelmed by the sheer volume of literature and "jargon" associated with these improved programming practices. Though certainly

1

not familiar with the intimate details of what lies behind some of this technology, phrases such as structured programming, top-down design, stepwise refinement, program design language, HIPO charts, chief programmer teams, program development libraries, structured walkthroughs and many others will be very familiar to most programmers. Before presenting an overview of some of the available tools and techniques, it is important to discuss and fully appreciate the nature of the problems facing programming professionals today.

1.2 SOFTWARE DEVELOPMENT PROBLEMS

It is a measure of the depth of the software crisis that we can confidently predict that every practicing programmer has been involved in the development of a software system that has gone awry for one reason or another. It is probable that the system suffered from a combination of the following common maladies:

(a)   Missed project deadlines, late system delivery
(b)   High development costs, budgets exceeded
(c)   User dissatisfaction, system performs inadequately or does not meet user requirements
(d)   Error-prone and unreliable, requiring excessive corrective maintenance
(e)   Overly-complex, difficult and expensive to perform adaptive maintenance.

Some of the major problems impacting software development are described in the remainder of this section.

Complexity

The fall in hardware costs and developments in hardware technology have made feasible increasingly ambitious projects and generated an almost insatiable demand for complex, sophisticated software. This trend will continue as we move from isolated stand-alone systems to integrated systems and as computing makes inroads into hitherto untapped application areas. The complex and intricate nature of these advanced software systems is often underestimated by project managers and results in wildly optimistic cost and time estimates. The design and implementation of these systems is carried out in an environment where costly time delays must be anticipated. Software systems evolve over time. Initial requirements specifications are often vague and incomplete, they need to be modified as the project proceeds. Additionally, the user may clarify, change, or add functional requirements. These modifications are all sources of delay and increased cost.

The design of complex software systems remains a fundamental problem despite the advances that have been made in software technology. There is no well-defined recipe which, if followed, guarantees a good design. Software design is an intellectually challenging and creative human task. Inventive, experienced designers are priceless assets of any programming shop. Whilst recognizing the importance of skilled individuals it has become increasingly evident that designers need helpful tools and techniques if they are to master the complexity of large scale application systems. When application systems were such that a small number of individuals might assume complete responsibility for the design and implementation of a system, software design tended to be a rather undisciplined process. Little distinction was made between design and programming. Programmers considered time spent on design as largely unproductive, believing that design and detailed coding were the same and could be performed concurrently. When applied to the design of large scale systems involving teams of programmers and hundreds of interacting program modules this *ad hoc* approach has proved disastrous. There are now, however, numerous useful tools and techniques which can assist programmers in the battle against complexity and which, when carefully selected and used in the right combination, can bring much needed discipline to the software development process.

Maintenance

Another daunting problem facing data processing installations is that each new application system put into operation immediately generates its own maintenance workload. In many installations 60 per cent or more of the workload is taken up with the maintenance of existing systems. This leaves fewer resources available for the development of new systems. New staff must be recruited or new developments delayed. Maintenance may be broadly classified into two types:

Adaptive maintenance

(a) to meet changes in the application environment, e.g. a change in taxation regulations
(b) to meet changes in the operation environment, e.g. the installation of a new compiler
(c) to satisfy requests from users for enhancements or modifications to a system.

Corrective maintenance

(a) to identify the cause of and correct bugs not discovered during system testing, i.e. repairing unreliable and non-robust software
(b) to improve a poorly performing system.

In many programming installations there has been a tendency to regard maintenance as a training ground for raw, inexperienced recruits freeing the more experienced programmers for more attractive, creative development work on new application systems. Maintenance has been seen as an activity requiring little skill. In fact, maintenance is a difficult task requiring high levels of skill, creativity and experience. What makes the task of the maintenace programmer so difficult?

The maintenance programmer must be able to quickly understand what the major functions of a program are and how these functions are accomplished. This is made more difficult because programs are poorly documented, poorly organized and the program code reflects the individual style and favorite programming "tricks" of the original program author.

Most programs requiring maintenance will already have undergone numerous modifications. Each modification makes the next one more difficult. The quality of a program's documentation, structure and reliability declines over the life of the program.

Designing a program so that it can be maintained easily is difficult. Unfortunately, ease of maintenance is often not a major consideration in the mind of a program designer. Consequently maintenance programmers find that programs do not accommodate changes easily. Modifications are not localized, they impact on seemingly unrelated parts of the program and cannot be implemented without major surgery on the structure of the program. Rather than carry out this time-consuming restructuring it is commonplace for the maintenance programmer to succumb to the temptation to implement the change with a "quick and dirty" fix or patch.

Management

The problems that beset software development are divided between those that are technical in nature and those that are caused by poor management. When software projects were small and project teams consisted of only a few people, informal methods of project planning and maintenance were adequate. For large complex projects, a formal integrated approach to management is necessary for successful project implementation. Some of the consequences of ineffective management are listed below:

(a)   poor estimating of project schedules leading to missed deadlines and late system delivery
(b)   poor cost estimation and management leading to budget overruns
(c)   poor project visibility making it impossible to assess the progress of the project and identify schedule slippages and trouble spots
(d)   ineffective project monitoring leading to a lack of adherence to

installation standards and poor discipline in using software tools and techniques

(e)   poor personnel management and ineffective communication channels.

In this text we concentrate our discussion on how these modern project management techniques affect the work of the programming practitioner.

Education

The demand for new application systems, fuelled by the fall in hardware costs, increased hardware capability, and increased user requirements, has created an acute shortage of skilled personnel. Data processing installations find themselves caught in a software cost spiral. New application systems are more complex than existing systems and therefore require more software development time. Once implemented, new systems are added to the existing software needing to be maintained. Systems now more rapidly reach the stage where they become too expensive to maintain and need to be completely replaced: the consequences of this are that the supply of suitably trained personnel entering the industry is inadequate to meet the demand, and that intense competition exists for the skills of the more experienced and talented professionals. Skilled programmers are able to command good salaries and change jobs easily.

The problems for those who manage software development projects have been compounded by the fact that only marginal improvements in software productivity have been achieved in recent years. Although individual programmer productivity varies greatly, rates of fewer than ten lines of finished code per day are commonplace. There are many factors which influence productivity but the sheer size and complexity of today's application systems are among the most significant. Most software practitioners have received little or no training in how to deal with these problems. For many, their only course in programming will have emphasized mastering the intricacies of a particular programming language rather than the fundamentals of problem solving, program design and coding techniques. Even fewer will have received any formal education in such desirable areas as design methodologies, communication skills, or the ergonomics or human factors involved in designing computer systems. Prior to entering the workplace it is unlikely that they will have been involved in the design and implementation of a large software system or in working within a project team. Fortunately, today's computer science graduates are generally far better prepared to meet the challenges of the data processing industry than their predecessors. For those overworked practitioners already in the field the acquisition of modern software skills is a slow and difficult process. Often new ideas are misunderstood and the implementation of new practices meets with considerable resistance.

1.3   MODERN PROGRAMMING PRACTICES

In this section we present an overview of recent major developments in software technology.

Structured Programming

The first use of the term *structured programming* can be traced back to the work of Dijkstra in the mid-1960s. Since then it has become one of those terms which means all things to all men. Structured programming, as first enunciated by Dijkstra,[1] does not lend itself to a rigid precise definition although many attempts at such definitions exist in the literature.

The major principles of structured programming can be summarized as follows:

(a)   A recognition that programming is a complex, intellectual activity and that we can no longer rely on idiosyncratic methods of program construction.

(b)   The introduction of organization and discipline into the programming process to master this complexity and attain the goals of correct, reliable and maintainable programs.

(c)   Program design is a distinct activity from coding and should be carried out in a systematic fashion using the following broad guidelines:

   (i)   The initial refinement of a problem decomposes it into a number of highly abstracted subordinate problems. Each of these are then themselves refined in a similar way into a set of less abstracted problems. This process, known as successive or stepwise refinement, continues until the problem solution is described at a level where translation into the required programming language can be achieved easily. This method of program design is known as top-down design and results in a hierarchic or tree-structured solution.

   (ii)   The transition between levels of refinement is kept as small as possible in order that each step can be understood easily and the correctness of the solution at each level can be informally verified.

   (iii)   During program design and coding only three basic control structures, sequence, selection, and repetition are generally necessary.

Although they leave many practical implementation issues unanswered these principles capture the spirit of the early pioneers of structured programming.

The advent of structured programming was the cause of widespread controversy amongst the programming community. Much of the controversy was the result of grossly oversimplifying the ideas being put forward and misunderstanding their true objectives. Two of the more common misconceptions are discussed below.

A widespread misconception was that structured programming could be equated to programming using only a restricted set of control structures and avoiding, at all costs, the use of the unconditional branch or **go to** statement. This narrow view of structured programming generated a heated debate as to whether the **go to** statement should be banished from high level programming languages and deflected attention from the main issue of how to design programs systematically.

Other programmers equated structured programming with modular programming. This technique arose as an alternative to the early common method of designing and coding programs in a monolithic fashion. Broadly stated, modular programming is the partitioning of a program into functionally independent modules. Provided the interface between modules is well defined, each module can be designed, coded, and tested independently, perhaps by different programmers. Few programmers argued with these ideas and saw structured programming as simply a restatement of the principles of modular programming. Today, modular programming is seen as a valuable component, but only a component, of structured programming. It lacks the discipline of structured programming in a number of areas, notably on how design is to be carried out within individual modules.

Structured programming inspired a resurgence of interest in the programming process. This has led to the development of a wide range of tools and techniques which have enabled the principles of structured programming to be put into practice in the workplace. In particular, guidelines have been proposed for the implementation of structured programs in COBOL, still by far the most predominantly used programming language for data processing applications. Also, a number of design methodologies have been developed and new project documentation and management techniques proposed. The term structured programming is now often used to refer collectively to the whole plethora of tools and techniques which have evolved from the initial ideas.

Design Methods and Principles

In recent years a number of approaches have been proposed to systematize the program design process. They are extensions and elaborations of Dijkstra's basic structured programming principles. Some approaches have been developed to the stage where they consist of an integrated collection of methods and principles and form the basis of a methodology for program design. The three design methodologies most used in the workplace are *Functional Decomposition*, *Data Flow Design* and *Data Structure Design*. Each methodology has its own strengths and weaknesses, and some are best applied to particular types of problem or to particular application areas. No preferred, generally applicable methodology has emerged or can be expected to emerge in the near future.

Two principles, top-down design and modularity, underly most of the methodologies. *Top-down design* (Wirth[2], Mills[3]) starts from a problem specification and generates a hierarchic or tree structured design through the process known as successive or stepwise refinement as described earlier. Each level of refinement of the design corresponds to a particular level of understanding of *what* the program has to do, independently of *how* the result will be achieved at lower levels of refinement. The method advocates that initial levels should concentrate on critical broad design issues and that details should be postponed until lower levels. This is in contrast to bottom-up design, a technique often associated with early versions of modular programming. *Bottom-up design* again results in a hierarchic solution structure but in this case the lower level detailed modules are identified and refined first and subsequently used as a foundation on which to build the design. In practice, design is never solely top-down or bottom-up but rather a combination of the two. In this text we adopt the view of most of the popular methodologies that design should be predominantly top-down but it may be necessary at certain times to practice bottom-up design to examine the feasibility of some low-level module before design can proceed.

The decomposition of a problem into well-defined modules is a powerful tool in the fight against complexity. A "separation of concerns" can be achieved which allows each module to be understood independently, the impact of design modifications localized to as few modules as possible (preferably one), and modules to be developed independently. An important principle known as *data hiding* or *encapsulation* (Parnas[4]) can assist in realizing the benefits of modularity. It suggests that each module should be constructed so that the function it accomplishes and the interface information required to use it are clearly visible but that the internal code and data structures used may be hidden away inside the module in the sense that they need not be known to utilize the module. That is, *what* the module does is clearly visible but *how* the module accomplishes its function should not be. In particular, each data structure (or file structure) involved in a program system should have the structure itself, the statements that access it, and the statements that modify it, enclosed in a single module.

The major difference between methodologies can often be identified by examining the technique each uses to decide how refinements are to be made at each level of a design. Three major schools of thought have emerged. Functional Decomposition suggests that design decisions should focus on the operations which need to be performed to solve a problem. Data Flow Design suggests that an analysis of the flow of data is of paramount importance whilst Data Structure Design suggests that the program structure should be derived from the data structures involved in a problem.

Functional Decomposition has been adopted by IBM as a constituent part of its collection of tools and techniques called *Improved Programming Technologies* (IPT). Each tool and technique can be used in isolation but users have achieved greatet success by carefully selecting a subset of them which complement and support each other. IPT provides tools and techniques to aid the design, implementation, and documentation of software projects and also introduces suggested management practices.

Program design is carried out in a predominantly top-down fashion. The main design objective is to achieve a modular solution structure largely based on functional decomposition of the problem. Implementation and testing is often carried out concurrently with design using a technique known as *Top-down Implementation* (TDI). The basic principle is that coding and testing should be performed as the design evolves rather than after the design stage has been completed. For example, once the highest level components of a program system are identified they are coded and tested before further lower level components are designed. The "top" of the system can be tested using throwaway program stubs or dummy modules to stand in for invoked, but as yet unwritten, lower level components. When invoked a program stub performs a much simplified version of the eventual program component. When the next level of design is complete, components will be coded to replace the stubs and immediately integrated into the evolving program to be tested, again using stubs to stand in for unwritten components where necessary.

This method for implementation and testing is in stark contrast to methods usually associated with implementations of modular programming where it was expected that the complete design process would be completed before implementation and testing would begin. Furthermore, implementation and testing began with the lowest level components. These were then tested using a "test harness" program to invoke the component under test in a way compatible with its eventual role in the complete system. Implementation and testing would then proceed bottom-up, integrating higher level components on top of those previously tested and again writing a test harness to carry out integration and testing. There are many other possible alternative procedures for implementation and testing. One method is to complete the design before carrying out implementation and testing top-down. A full discussion of these issues is found in Chapter 11.

Also at IBM, a software design method known initially as *Structured Design* was developed by Yourdon and Constantine.[5] The method has been extended by Yourdon and Myers[6] and is now also known by the names *Transform-centred Design*, *Composite Design*, or most commonly *Data Flow Design*. The method chiefly concerns itself with how programs should be decomposed into modules and what criteria can be used to evaluate the quality of a program design. A basic principle of the method is that an analysis of the flow of data in a problem and the transformations that are applied to this data is essential to achieve a good design. Two important concepts, cohesion and coupling, are introduced as measures to be used when evaluating a potential design. Cohesion is a measure of the relationships that exist between elements within a particular module. Coupling is a measure of the relationships that exist between modules. It is suggested that modules should be weakly coupled but strongly cohesive.

Data Structure Design is a method for program design, developed by Jackson,[7] which has its roots in the United Kingdom but has achieved extensive use in Europe and the United States in recent years. The method concentrates almost solely on program design and has proved to be most appropriate when applied to the design of file processing applications systems. The basic principle on which the method stands is that the program structure which evolves from program design must reflect the problem structure and that this can best be achieved by using the data structures involved in a problem as a basis for the program design. In its simplest form the basic technique is as follows:

(a)   Define the input and output data structures involved in the problem. Generate a hierarchical data structure diagram for each input and output data structure by applying the principle of decomposition to the data involved.
(b)   Create an outline hierarchical structure based on all the data structures.
(c)   List the elementary operations that the program must perform and allocate each of them to a component in the program structure.

The method identifies two situations where the complexity of a problem may cause difficulties in the basic method. For example, a technique known as program inversion is proposed for cases where no single program structure can be found which matches all the data structures. A full discussion of the method can be found in Jackson.[7] Warnier[8] has developed a design methodology known as the *Logical Construction of Programs* which also adopts the data structure approach to program design and is similar in many ways to the Jackson method.

Documentation Tools

As new methods for program design have emerged so have new graphic aids to help document designs. Some are designed to support a particular design methodology whilst others are more generally applicable.

The traditional documentation tool for detailed program design is the *flowchart*. Since the advent of structured programming the flowchart has steadily lost popularity. Documentation tools which are less unwieldy to use and are more in tune with modern ideas of program structure and design have emerged.

Pseudocode, structured English, or *Program Design Language* (PDL)[9] is a formalization of natural language which is increasingly being used for detailed program design. Many variations of pseudocode exist; there is no accepted standard. Natural language is used to express design thoughts and a set of high level language-like control structures are used to allow specification of the design logic. Control constructs are usually chosen to be as close as possible to those provided by the target programming language into which the design will ultimately be coded.

The hierarchic or tree structure which results from the use of functional decomposition and top-down design can be illustrated using charts known variously as hierarchy, structure or *visual table of contents* (VTOC) charts. These charts illustrate the levels of refinement of the design and the inter-dependencies of modules within the design. VTOC charts are part of a documentation package from IBM known as HIPO charts.[10] HIPO charts, an acronym for Hierarchy plus Input, Process, Output charts, consist of a series of diagrams which document the top-down design of a program system at various levels of detail.

Management and Organizational Tools

It has become increasingly evident that poor project management and organizational methods have been significant factors in the failures of many software projects. To improve project management control and increase project visibility a number of techniques have been introduced to organize project teams. The techniques address two major problems which arise when programmers work in teams. Firstly, how to prevent the overhead of communication between team members from overwhelming the project. Secondly, how to allocate the project workload amongst team members to ensure that productivity is maximized.

The *Chief Programmer Team* concept[11,12] is a constituent part of IBM's package of Improved Programming Technologies. Chief Programmer Teams reduce communication between team members by organizing the team into a hierarchical working and reporting structure. Tasks are allocated amongst team members by separating out well defined roles for each individual and ensuring that each member is allocated tasks commensurate with their level of skill, specialist knowledge and experience. The Chief Programmer, the most highly skilled and experienced team member, acts as coordinator for the project. His or her role is technical; a project manager looks after the administration of the project. The Chief Programmer is normally personally responsible for certain areas of the project, for example, the top level design, and also allocates tasks to team members. To support the operation of the team, a *Program Production Library* maintains a record of all human machine-readable material relevant to the project. The use of the library has two main benefits. The status of the project at any time is more publicly visible and programmers are freed from some of the more clerical tasks they would normally perform, allowing them more time for tasks which require their specialist programming skills. A librarian is responsible for the upkeep of the project documentation within the library and acts as a technical secretary to team members carrying out such activities as keypunching, program editing, job preparation and submission of program runs.

Structured Walkthroughs (Yourdon[13]) are organized meetings at which a review of some component of a project is carried out. They are used to review work carried out at all stages of a project but have proved most successful when used to examine the quality of program designs and code. The programmer or designer whose work is under review walks through or guides the reviewers through the design or code. The reviewers, who have received the review material in advance, endeavor to detect design faults, program bugs, inadequate testing etc. Correction of any faults discovered is the responsibility of the reviewee. Any undetected faults are the responsibility of the entire review team. To maintain an informal and cordial atmosphere, management do not normally attend walkthroughs and they should not be used as a basis for employee evaluation. When successfully implemented, programmers tend to lose any apprehension they may feel about having their work publicly exposed and the technique can stimulate a friendly team spirit and create a more enjoyable working environment. Successful users of walkthroughs claim improvements in software quality, programmer productivity, programmer morale, programmer expertise, and meeting of deadlines.

1.4   ORGANIZATION AND CONTENT OF THE BOOK

In this chapter we have reviewed the problems currently facing the data processing industry and presented an overview of some of the modern programming practices which have been proposed to deal with them. In the remainder of this text we present a detailed look at a carefully chosen set of tools and techniques which can either be used individually or alternatively can be thought of as collectively forming an integrated programming methodology. Of course, we cannot claim to have solved all of the problems of the business application programmer in the chapters that follow. A "complete" and "correct" programming methodology remains to be discovered. A vast array of tools and techniques have been suggested to improve the programming process in some way or other. It would not be meaningful to attempt to discuss them all in a single text. Those programming practices discussed in this text were chosen according to the following criteria: their general applicability to the business application programmer, the degree to which they have been field tested, evidence of their acceptance and usefulness from user surveys and whether or not they form a coherent set of tools and techniques.

The most critical components of any methodology are those dealing with program design. Of the many suggested program design methodologies, the three that have received most attention are Functional Decomposition, Data Flow Design and Data Structure Design. The texts by Yourdon and Constantine[5] and Jackson[7] fully describe the Data Flow Design and Data Structure Design methods respectively and we will therefore not discuss these methods as such in the remainder of this text. We will present a design methodology which we will refer to by the name Top Down Stepwise Refinement and which is centred around the concept of Functional Decomposition, although we will make use of concepts from other methodologies where appropriate.

The objective of the text is to present these modern programming practices from the viewpoint of the impact they will have on the business application programmer. In initial chapters we develop the program design methodology and illustrate its use with detailed case studies of typical business application programs. Subsequently we discuss how program designs may be transformed into well-structured, reliable COBOL programs. In later chapters we discuss approaches to the implementation and testing of program systems and describe the impact on programmers of approaches for the organization and management of software projects.

1.5 REFERENCES

1. Dijkstra, E. W. "Notes on Structured Programming", *Structured Programming*, O. J. Dahl, E. W. Dijkstra and C. A. R. Hoare, Academic Press, London, 1972.

2. Wirth, N. "Program Development by Stepwise Refinement", *Comm. ACM*, **14** (4), 1971.

3. Mills, H. D. "Top Down Programming in Large Systems" in *Debugging Techniques in Large Systems*, Prentice-Hall, Englewood Cliffs, N.J., pp.44–55, 1971.

4. Parnas, D. L. "On the Criteria to be used in Decomposing Systems into Modules", *Comm. ACM*, **15** (12), 1972.

5. Yourdon, E. and Constantine, L. L. *Structured Design*, Prentice-Hall, Englewood Cliffs, N.J., 1979.

6. Myers, G. J. *Reliable Software through Composite Design*, Petrocelli/Charter, New York, 1975.

7. Jackson, M. A. *Principles of Program Design*, Academic Press, London, 1975.

8. Warnier, J. D. *Logical Construction of Programs*, Van Nostrand Reinhold, New York, 1974.

9. Caine, S. H. and Gordon, E. K. "PDL-A Tool for Software Design", *Proc. AFIPS* 1975 *NCC*, pp.271–276.

10. *HIPO–A Design Aid and Documentation Technique*, IBM Report No. GX20–1851, Oct. 1974.

11. Baker, F. T. "Chief Programmer Team Management of Production Programming", *IBM Systems Journal*, No. 1, 1972.

12. Baker, F. T. and Mills, H. D. "Chief Programmer Teams", *Datamation*, **19** (12), 1973.

13. Yourdon, E., *Structured Walkthroughs* (2nd ed.), Prentice-Hall, Englewood Cliffs, N.J., 1979.

2

Structured Program Design

2.1 INTRODUCTION

Chapter 1 discussed many of the problems which make the development of "good" software such a difficult task. To improve the software production process, tools, techniques, and organizational methods are needed for every aspect of the development cycle. In this chapter we tackle probably the programmer's most fundamental problem. How should programs be designed? Most programmers have probably received little formal guidance on this subject. It is only in recent years that universities, colleges, and commercial organizations have begun to focus attention on teaching the fundamentals of program design as well as familiarizing students with the syntax and semantics of particular programming languages. The design techniques used by programmers are often self-taught; the result of analyzing their own mistakes, and sharing the experiences of their colleagues.

As software systems became larger and more complex the need for an organized approach to program design became critical. The absence of such an approach led to:

(a) programs which reflected the individual approach of the designer, resulting in programs that are difficult to understand by anyone other than their author

(b) programs which are expensive to maintain and difficult to adapt to even small changes in the program requirements

(c) programs whose correctness is difficult to demonstrate.

Programmers today are exhorted to produce programs which have many, if not all, of the following qualities:

(a)   easily maintained and adaptable to change
(b)   reliable and robust
(c)   understandable
(d)   efficient in terms of their resource demands
(e)   delivered on time.

How are programs with these qualities to be achieved? We believe that program design is the most crucial stage in a program's development and that decisions taken at this time will ultimately decide whether these objectives will be realized. If a poor design is not detected until the testing stage of a program, redesign, with all that that implies, is the only effective remedy. Additional time spent at the design stage of a program will be saved many times over during debugging and testing. The motto must be "design first—code later", no matter how much we feel the need to actually get some code written.

If program design is not to remain a completely intuitive process, what tried and tested techniques are available for use? During recent years a number of program design methodologies have evolved to try and bridge the gap between program specification and program. Even so, program design necessarily remains a creative process. The methodologies provide a framework within which the chances of creating a quality program are greatly enhanced, but original thought still has a major role to play.

It is not our intention to discuss the relative merits of these methodologies. The interested reader is referred to the works of Dijkstra,[1,2] Jackson[3] and Yourdon and Constantine[4] in particular. A suggested reading list appears at the end of this chapter. In this text we present a methodology which is based on the concept of Functional Decomposition but which encompasses features from a number of methodologies. We will refer to this general methodology as the Top-down Stepwise Refinement method.

In this chapter we will study the fundamental principles of this method before applying it to the design of several typical data processing problems in succeeding chapters. Chapter 4 examines the program design process in more detail and offers further advice as to how best to organize program design.

2.2   THE TOP-DOWN STEPWISE REFINEMENT METHOD

The fundamental principle of the method we present is that program design should proceed in a *top-down* manner. Using the program specification as a starting point, we should initially identify the major sequence of tasks which the program is to perform so that we may establish the overall or top-level logic of the required program. It is important at this stage to concentrate our attention on *what* the major functions of the program are, rather than on *how* these functions are to be realized. For example, if we were designing a simple sales summary report program, we might use the abstract statement:

    generate report

to convey the overall task to be accomplished by the program. An initial design step might be to partition this task into a sequence of three subtasks as follows:

    initialize report
    process each sales record
    output sales summary statistics

Each of these three tasks would then be expressed in more detail in a similar way. The program design continues as a series of refinements to the currently existing design. The design proceeds on a level-by-level basis where each level of refinement expresses the program design in progressively increasing levels of detail. This process continues until no further refinement is possible, that is, when the solution is expressed at a level of detail compatible with the primitives provided by a high level programming language, in our case COBOL.

The program design process can be usefully represented as an evolving structure of hierarchy chart. These charts are also often referred to as VTOC (Visual Table Of Contents) charts which themselves are a constituent part of a larger documentation package known as HIPO charts.[5]

The chart shown in Fig. 2.1 clearly shows the hierarchic structure which results from top-down design. Each block or component in the chart will ultimately be represented as an identifiable part of a program structure. This might be as a subprogram, group of paragraphs, or a single paragraph depending on the size of the component. The chart also displays the interdependencies of the components; the refinement of a particular function or component is represented by those components subordinate to it in the chart. The topmost levels of the chart express the solution in terms of only general functional requirements (*what* has to be done), whilst the lower levels contain increasing amounts of implementation detail (*how* it is to be done). The structure chart is a good medium for documenting the hierarchic or architectural structure of a program design. Note, however, that it does not provide information as to the order in which components in the chart are to be executed.

Our discussion of the method thus far has dictated that program design should result in a set of hierarchically ordered components. We adopt a "divide and conquer" approach to help manage the complexity of the

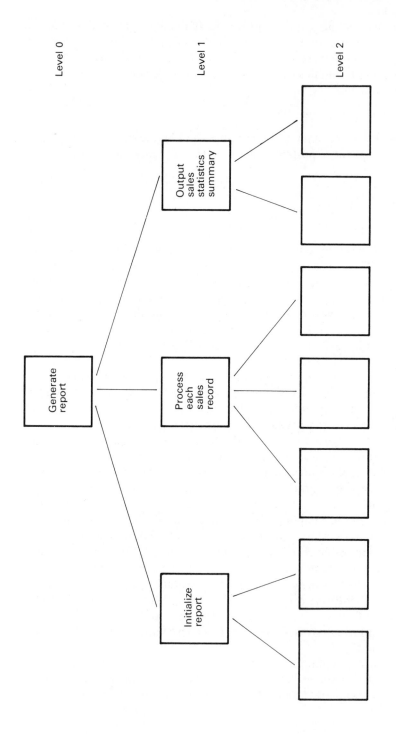

Fig. 2.1 A visual table of contents chart.

programming process and attempt to defer design details until we reach a stage in the design process at which their consideration is more appropriate. Clearly, in order to achieve a readable, maintainable, and reliable program, many other factors need to be considered. For example, the degree of functional independence between components in our design will have a major bearing on whether we achieve these qualities or not. Each component in our design should perform an identifiable, independent task. Avoid distributing a function amongst several components. It will then be easier to isolate the cause of, and to remedy, any problems that may arise with a particular functional component. This avoids the "ripple" effect where small changes made to one component affect many other components. Also if we wish to extend the program in some way, it is then easier to replace one component by another because the original is independent and self-contained. Further discussion of the many other factors relating to "good" program design will be delayed until we have studied an initial example in Chapter 3.

The following questions illustrate some of the problems which, as yet, remain unanswered:

(a) In what order should components in our design be refined?
(b) When exactly does a "what" become a "how"?
(c) When many refinements of a component are possible, how are we to decide which refinement is the "best"?
(d) How are individual components to be structured?
(e) What constitutes a good component? How big or small should a component be?
(f) Is strictly top-down design a practical proposition?
(g) How do we ensure the correctness of every stage in our program design?

2.3 LOGIC STRUCTURES

The structure charts we have discussed illustrate the hierarchical relationships between components but do not express the detailed logic nor the order in which the components are to be executed. We will use an informal language known as *pseudocode* to act both as a design aid and as documentation for this part of the program development process.

First we discuss guidelines for the construction of components in our design. These guidelines have evolved from the pioneering work of Dijkstra,[1,2] Wirth,[6] Mills,[7] Bohm and Jacopini[8] and the subsequent contributions of many other researchers.

The first use of the now common term "structured programming" is attributable to Dijkstra with his now famous paper *Goto Statement Considered Harmful* and his subsequent treatise *Notes on Structured Programming*. Although the debate over whether or not the **go to** (i.e. arbitrary branch) statement should be used dominated the discussion relating to structured programming for many years, Dijkstra's main tenet was that we should adopt methods which enable us to make programs more manageable by reducing complexity. This can be achieved by introducing organization and discipline into the programming process.

One facet of structured programming is that wherever possible we should avoid the use of unconditional transfers of control as their use leads to code which is often unnecessarily difficult to follow. Rather, we should use control structures which enable programs to be written so that the structure of the source text will reflect the dynamic behavior of the program when it is executed. Bohm and Jacopini[8] proved mathematically that it is possible to write programs of any size and complexity using only a restricted set of three structured control constructs:

Sequence   —components are to be executed in the order in which they appear.
Selection   —a two-way decision structure.
Repetition   —a condition-controlled looping mechanism.

Mills[7] extended this result to show that if we introduce the additional constraint that all program components should have one entry and one exit it becomes easier to prove the correctness of programs. Note that each of the three logic constructs satisfy the one entry, one exit rule. Although the day when we will be able to prove the correctness of our programs is still a long way away, many other benefits accrue from adopting this approach.

Theoretically, we need only these three basic logic constructs. In practice however, it is necessary to expand this set, but each additional construct must still satisfy the one entry, one exit constraint. In this regard, we will introduce an alternative decision structure which allows the selection of one from many, rather than two, alternatives.

In both our program design and code we will initially adopt the following rule:

All program components will be constructed using only sequence, selection or repetition structures or combinations of these.

Since each of the primitive structures has one entry and one exit, this rule will ensure that all program components share this property. This rule blends in particularly well with the ideas of top-down design and results in programs:

(a)   which are hierarchically structured into functional components

(b)   where the logic for each component will flow from the beginning to the
      end of the component without arbitrary branching and will therefore
      be more readable and understandable.

(c)   where the static logic structures reflect the dynamic behavior of the
      program.

2.4 PSEUDOCODE

How are we to document the development of our program design? The
traditional design aid and documentation tool is the flowchart. However, the
popularity of the flowchart has declined in recent years due to the emergence
of tools which are more compatible with the ideas of structured programming.

In particular, flowcharts have the following disadvantages:

(a)   They are awkward and time-consuming to draw and difficult to main-
      tain. Indeed, many programmers use them only to placate the insati-
      able appetite of their managers for documentation.

(b)   Many programmers do not draw the flowchart until after the program
      has been debugged and tested. The flowcharts are therefore not pro-
      duced concurrently with the program design. One reason for this is that
      in their simplest form they offer no positivie help when designing a
      program; the primitive logic constructs they provide are conditional
      and unconditional branch structures and labels.

(c)   Even when a program is well-structured, flowcharts tend to conceal
      rather than display this structure.

The flowchart itself has been adapted to meet more adequately the
needs of structured programming. Some programming installations make
use of "structured" flowcharts[9] where only a subset of flowchart structures
are permitted (sequence, selection and repetition). In this text we will make
use of an increasingly popular documentation and design tool known variously as pseudocode, structured English, pidgin English, or program design
language.

Pseudocode is an informal language; it cannot be compiled, and is
largely independent of any programming language. No "standard"
pseudocode exists but differences in variations are normally minimal.
Pseudocode is a mixture of natural language, which we use to express our
design thoughts, and structured control statements which specify the logic
flow and the hierarchic design structure in an unambiguous manner. It may
be stored conveniently in machine-readable form and hence maintained
easily using a text editor. Syntactic rules are kept to a minimum, though

keywords are used to specify flow of control and indentation rules are used to highlight the logic structure. The natural language used allows the programmer to express his design at a level of completeness and detail appropriate to the current point in the development of a design solution. As the program design develops so the pseudocode and level of detail within it will expand. The pseudocode acts naturally as documentation for the design thought process.

The pseudocode presented in this text is particularly appropriate for a COBOL installation though we will be careful to ensure that it is free from any of the idiosyncracies of the language. First we examine how the three basic logic structures will be represented.

The most fundamental of all logic constructs is the sequence. It simply means that program components are to be executed in the order in which they are written. In pseudocode this is stated by writing the "English" description for each component one after the other.

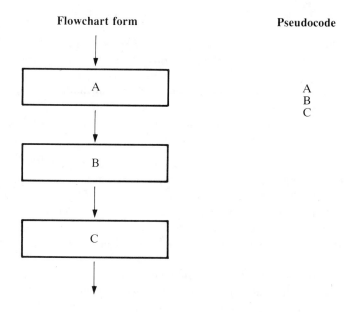

You will recall that in the discussion of the Top-down Stepwise Refinement method we suggested that when designing a simple sales summary report we might use the abstract statement generate report to represent the task to be accomplished by the program. We then proceeded to partition this task into three subtasks. In pseudocode this would be represented:

generate report
  initialize report
  process each sales record
  output sales summary statistics

In the example we have introduced notation and indentation rules. To indicate that we are describing the decomposition of generate report we indent the decomposition underneath its paragraph header. To indicate that *initialize report, process each sales record*, etc. are not primitive components we write them in *italics*. A primitive component is defined as a component which has been refined to the point where it can be readily translated into program code. The elaboration of each non-primitive is described in a separate paragraph.

The pseudocode is therefore:

generate report
  initialize report
  process each sales record
  output sales summary statistics

initialize report
  .
  .
  .

process each sales record
  .
  .
  .

output sales summary statistics
  .
  .
  .

You will notice that the pseudocode structure strongly resembles the paragraph structure of COBOL's PROCEDURE DIVISION.

The simplest selection structure allows us to select one of two components based on the evaluation of a condition. In pseudocode we introduce the structured keywords **if, then, else** and **endif** to construct selection structures.

Flowchart form   **Pseudocode**

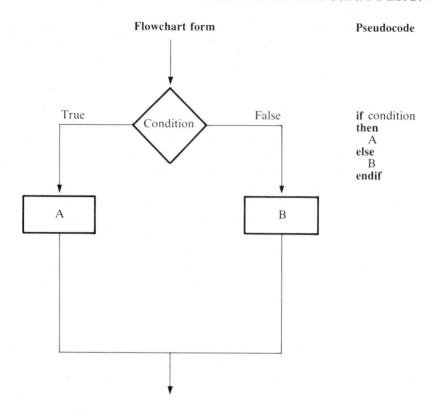

if condition
then
    A
else
    B
endif

The **endif** keyword acts as a terminator to indicate the end of the scope of the selection structure. We introduce further notation and indentation rules here: all keywords will be written in **bold face** and the constituent parts of the selection structure will be aligned and indented as shown to highlight the logical structure.

A simpler version of the selection structure appears when the choice is one of performing an action or not. In this case the selection structure has the form:

if condition
then
    A
endif

Repetition is used to execute a function repeatedly until a condition becomes true. In pseudocode we will use the keywords **perform** and **until** to construct repetition structures.

Flowchart form   **Pseudocode**

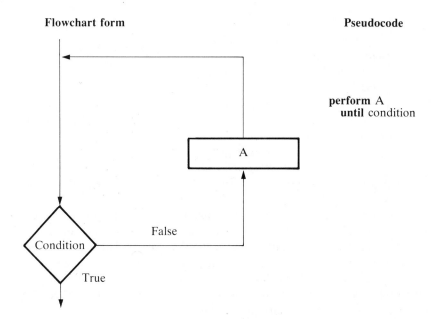

perform A
    until condition

The flowchart form of the structure clearly shows that **perform...until** is a leading decision looping mechanism, and therefore the function A may never be performed if the condition is initially true. We refer to this kind of mechanism as a zero or many times loop structure. Often this type of leading decision loop will be referred to as a **while...do** or **do...while** structure. As ultimately our pseudocode is to be translated into COBOL we will use COBOL reserved words PERFORM and UNTIL to increase the correspondence between pseudocode and COBOL code and also ease the translation process between the two. (COBOL statements will be written in upper case, in accordance with convention.)

We now have the three basic logic structures that are necessary to create well-structured programs. Each of the three structures may be nested within each other indefinitely. That is, whenever a function component appears in the three basic structures it may be replaced by any of the other structures. This is illustrated by the following program design fragment.

reorder stock items
    read a record from the stock file
    perform *analyze each stock record*
        until end of stock file reached
    halt

analyze each stock record
   if number in stock < reorder point
   then
      reorder this stock item
   endif
   read a record from the stock file

reorder this stock item
   calculate how many items to order
   find supplier of this stock item
   generate order and send to supplier

COBOL programmers will recognize this as a simple program design for processing a sequential file. The design of such programs will be considered in depth in later chapters. Several points are, however, worth noting from the example. As each of our basic logic structures is a one entry, one exit structure, nesting them within each other creates more complex logic structures that also have the one entry, one exit property. All paragraphs in our pseudocode will have this property as will the complete design. The first paragraph in the pseudocode will correspond to the initial decomposition in our design. It will therefore be the top level control component and "execution" of our pseudocode will always start and finish in this component.

Again, as recognition of the fact that we will always be producing COBOL programs, we make one further compromise to present-day COBOL in our pseudocode. As COBOL's PERFORM...UNTIL statement does not allow in-line coding, we will not use this in our pseudocode. Therefore, in our earlier example, instead of:

   perform
      if number in stock < reorder point
      then
         reorder this stock item
      endif
      read a record from stock file
   until end of stock file reached

we used

   perform *analyze each stock record*
      until end of stock file reached

where *analyze each stock record* described the functions to be repeated.
The definite advantage of enforcing this restriction is that now each

paragraph in our pseudocode will be matched with a corresponding paragraph in the COBOL program.

We stated earlier that theoretically only three basic logic structures were actually required to design and code our programs. This does not restrict us, however, from extending the set of allowed constructs where the need warrants and where the new logic construct has the one entry, one exit property we require.

We extend our pseudocode with a specialized selection structure to handle the commonly arising situation where we wish to choose one of any number of, rather than just two, functions depending on the value of some item. This alternative selection mechanism is universally known as a **case** structure.

The **case** structure is a multi-way selection structure. In our pseudocode we will use the keywords **case, of, else** and **endcase** to construct **case** structures. The structure is best illustrated using an example. In a validate or edit program almost always the validation tests we wish to perform on an input record will depend on the type of transaction involved. If there are many transaction types, the logic required to select the appropriate tests to be done is best represented using a **case** structure.

Pseudocode

```
case transaction type of
     addition:          validate addition transaction
     deletion:          validate deletion transaction
     change name:       validate name change
     change address:    validate address change
     else:              handle transaction type error
endcase
```

The meaning of this **case** structure is as follows. If the value of the transaction type is listed as one of the possible **case** values then the function corresponding to this label is selected. If not, the function corresponding to the **else** clause is selected. Fig. 2.2 clearly shows that the **case** is a one entry, one exit structure and also that one and only one of the **case** functions is ever selected.

We can generalize our example to allow any number of possible alternative functions to be specified. The **endcase** acts as a delimiter for the entire **case** structure and for the final **case** alternative. Every other **case** structure is delimited by the **case** value for the next alternative. The **else** clause is optional; in the situation where it is not specified and the value of the **case** item is not equal to any of the specified possible values, none of the **case** alternatives will be selected.

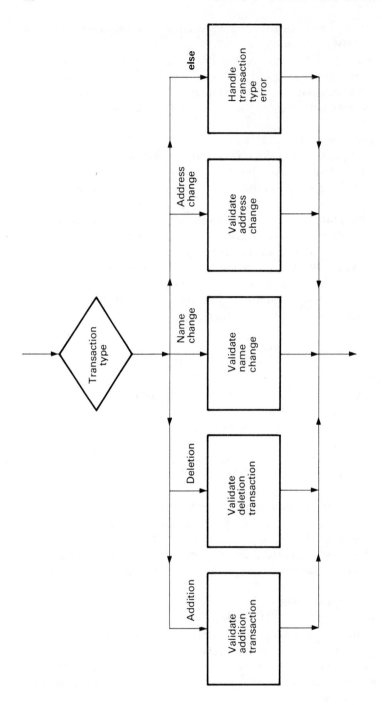

Fig. 2.2 Case structure.

In this book we use **bold** face to distinguish key words and *italics* to distinguish components that are to be broken down. Normally, of course, the programmer cannot use these special printers' facilities. Pseudocode usually remains in handwritten form. However, the different elements of pseudocode can be distinguished, for example, by writing key words in capitals, everything else in lower case, and underlining the name of components that are not primitive.

2.5 SUMMARY

In this chapter we discussed the need for an organized and disciplined approach to program design. In response to that need we presented a methodology for program design referred to as Top-down Stepwise Refinement.

The basic principles of the method are that:

(a)   design proceeds top-down
(b)   functional decomposition (*what* needs to be done) precedes detailed algorithm design (*how* it is to be done)
(c)   a hierarchically structured design is achieved by successively refining the design at any stage with increasing levels of detail
(d)   the hierarchic design structure and the design solution at each level of refinement can be documented using a hierarchy or structure chart
(e)   each component in the design performs an identified function and is as independent as possible from other components in the design.

In line with the ideas of structured programming the following rules were adopted for organizing the logic structures in a program design:

(a)   only three basic logic structures are allowed, sequence, selection (**if, case**), and repetition (**perform . . . until**)
(b)   only programs and program components which have one entry and one exit are allowed.

Pseudocode was introduced as an alternative to flowcharting in the documentation of a program design. The version of pseudocode presented is tailored so that eventual translation of a program design into COBOL is relatively trivial. Pseudocode implementations of the basic logic structures were described and guidelines were suggested for the presentation of designs in pseudocode to make them easier to read and understand.

2.6 REFERENCES AND FURTHER READING

1. Dijkstra, E. W., "Goto Statement Considered Harmful", Letter to Editor, *Comm. ACM*, **11** (3), pp.147–148.

2. Dijkstra, E. W., "Notes on Structured Programming", *Structured Programming*, O. J. Dahl, E. W. Dijkstra and C. A. R. Hoare, Academic Press, London, 1972.

3. Jackson, M. A., *Principles of Program Design*, Academic Press, London, 1975.

4. Yourdon, E. and Constantine, L. L., *Structured Design*, Prentice-Hall, Englewood Cliffs, N.J., 1979.

5. *HIPO – A Design Aid and Documentation Technique*, IBM Report No. GX20–1851, Oct. 1974.

6. Wirth, N., "Program Development by Stepwise Refinement", *Comm. ACM*, **14** (4), 1971.

7. Mills, H. D., "Top Down Programming in Large Systems" in *Debugging Techniques in Large Systems*, Prentice-Hall, Englewood Cliffs, N.J., pp.44–55, 1971.

8. Bohm, C. and Jacopini, G., "Flow Diagrams, Turing Machines and Languages with only Two Formation Rules, *Comm. ACM*, **9** (5), 1966.

9. Nassi, I. and Shneiderman, B., "Flowchart Techniques for Structured Programming", *ACM SIGPLAN Notices* **8**(8), Aug. 1973, pp.12–26.

10. Bergland, G. D., "A Guided Tour of Program Design Methodologies", *IEEE Computer*, pp.13–37, Oct. 1981.
    This article compares and evaluates four major program design methodologies. The essential characteristics of each methodology are identified by applying each methodology to the same example problem.

11. *Datamation*, December 1973 (issue on structured programming).
    An interesting series of articles providing an overview of structured programming.

12. Dijkstra, E. W., *A Discipline of Programming*, Prentice-Hall, Englewood Cliffs, N.J., 1976.
    This intellectually challenging text presents this respected author's insights into the discipline of program development. For the serious reader only.

3

The Design of a Report Program

3.1 INTRODUCTION

In this chapter we illustrate how the methodology for program design presented in Chapter 2 may be applied to the design of a typical data processing application program. Top-down Stepwise Refinement will be used to design a program which generates a monthly sales summary report. Studying this example will enable us to illustrate techniques for dealing with several problems that are fundamental to business data processing applications:

(a)   the design of programs which process sequentially organized input files
(b)   the extraction of summary information from such files
(c)   the production of multi-page reports where summary information is to be presented at various levels.

Even for relatively simple problems, program design is not as straightforward as text book solutions suggest. In the case studies presented in the following chapters we document as fully as possible the thought sequences which lead up to eventual design decisions. In some cases alternative designs will be documented and the rationale for choosing between them given. The reader should attempt the exercises provided at the end of this chapter. Many of the problems which are discussed in Chapter 4 will then have been encountered first hand.

3.2 THE PROGRAM SPECIFICATION

Before embarking on any detailed design activities it is important to study the program specification very carefully. We must ensure that we understand exactly the problem we are being asked to solve. Program specifications are not normally communicated from originator to programmer without some kind of clarification or discussion being necessary. It is preferable, and far less expensive, to discover any inconsistency or vagueness in the specification before any investment is made in the design and implementation of a solution. A specification for the summary report follows:

Computer run diagram:

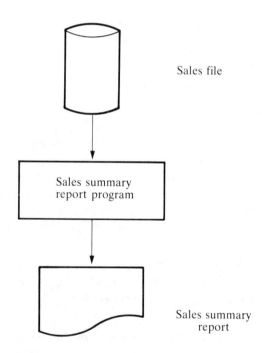

Sales file

Sales summary report program

Sales summary report

Program description:

The Nu-Wave Cosmetics Company maintains a sequentially organized file detailing each sale made by each of its salespersons during a particular month. The sales department of the company is divided into a number of sales territories, each of which is subdivided into a small number of sales areas. Within each area the company employs a team of sales personnel.

Nu-Wave requires a report which summarizes the monthly sales information as follows:

(a) for each sales area a summary is required which details the total sales made by each salesperson and the total sales for that area
(b) following the area summaries, an additional summary is required which details the monthly sales for each territory and the total monthly sales figure for the company as a whole.

Input file(s):

Sales file

(a) sequentially organized
(b) sorted by ascending salesperson number within ascending area within ascending territory
(c) each record in the file describes an individual sale by a sales employee and is formatted as shown below:

Territory-code	99 (Values 1 through 12)
Area-code	9
Salesperson-number	9(5)
Salesperson-name	X(30)
Sales-amount	9(5)V99

Output file(s):

Sales summary report

The sales summary report is to consist of:

(a) For each area a summary detailing individual salesperson totals and a total sales figure for the area. The required layout for the area summaries is shown below:

```
                    NU-WAVE COSMETICS
           MONTHLEY SALE SUMMARY REPORT              PAGE 1
TERRITORY 01                                         AREA 1
          SALESPERSON              MONTHLY SALES AMOUNT ($)
          00331 MS D FRITZ                 199.99
          00451 MS J SMITH                1200.00
          00739 MS F MALONE               7786.78
          00804 MS T NASH                 3199.99
            .     .                          .
            .     .                          .
            .     .                          .

               AREA TOTAL          $21386.76
```

(b)　A final summary is required which details the monthly sales for each territory and the total monthly sales for the company. The required layout is shown below:

NU-WAVE COSMETICS

MONTHLY SALES SUMMARY REPORT　　　　　PAGE 10

TERRITORY	SALES ($)
01	21386.76
03	9378.99
07	10996.54
.	.
.	.
.	.
.	.

TOTAL MONTHLY SALES　　　　　$134741.39

Program details:

(a)　the data in the sales file have been previously validated. No further error checking is necessary

(b)　sequence checking of the sales file is *not* required

(c)　the sales function is currently divided into 12 sales territories: the program should allow for future expansion to 20 territories

(d)　there will be no more than nine areas per territory

(e)　if an empty sales file is encountered the program should be aborted and the message "empty sales file encountered" displayed

(f)　a single output file is to be used to produce the sales summary report

(g)　the maximum number of salespersons in any given area is such that an area summary will not overflow a page boundary when salesperson total lines are single spaced

(h)　line formatting, line spacing and other report layout details are left to the discretion of the programmer. However, the information content and overall layout of the report is to follow the examples given.

3.3　INITIAL THOUGHTS

How should we begin? One of the fundamental principles of our method is that, in the initial stages of the design process, we should try and think in terms of very high level or abstract functions which the program must carry out. What we are attempting to do is to delay considering the details and intricacies of a problem until we reach a point in the design where they can be more appropriately considered. Initially therefore, we should be thinking of what functions are involved rather than how these functions are to be accomplished. Obtaining a clear idea of the inputs, functions and outputs of the program will be a good guide to determining the initial structure for a program design.

In the sales summary example the functions to be carried out are almost entirely governed by the structure of the sales details file being processed and the structure of the report being produced. A simple study of the specification shows that the two major functions of the program are:

(a)   to produce a separate summary report for each area
(b)   to produce a summary of monthly sales by territory.

It should be clear that the area summary reports can be produced as the records detailing sales for that area are accessed sequentially from the file. However, if the territory summary is to be generated as the last page of the report as specified in the program specification, territory information will need to be accumulated for use when the complete file of sales detail records has been processed.

If we refer to the overall function of the program by the abstract statement, *produce sales summary report*, an initial refinement of the design might be:

> *produce sales summary report*
> * extract summary information*
> * print territory summary*

In all programs that we design there will be various housekeeping activities to be done (e.g. opening and closing files). A more realistic initial decomposition is therefore:

> *produce sales summary report*
> * initialization*
> * extract summary information*
> * print territory summary*
> * termination*

We can think of *initialization*, *print territory summary* etc. as primitive functions of some powerful hypothetical virtual machine on which we are programming.

To proceed with the design we need to refine the components in our current solution. Which one should we consider first? This is an important question and will be discussed in greater detail in the next chapter. For the time being, we will adopt a simple "rule of thumb" and choose the component that seems to require the most consideration. This is clearly the component *extract summary information*. Refinement of this component will also help to define some of the functions to be carried out by *initialization* and *termination*.

We noticed earlier that we can produce the area summary reports as we process the sales details for that area from the file. This is possible because of the way in which the input file is ordered. We know that records in the file are sorted by salesperson number within area within territory.

The processing of records from a sequentially organized file is fundamental to many data processing applications. In the next section we consider how records from such a file should be processed before returning to our example.

3.4 PROCESSING A SEQUENTIAL FILE

The simplest strategy to adopt to process records from a sequential file is to read a record from the file, process it, read the next record, process it and so on. This gives a logic structure:

> **perform** *read and process records*
>   **until** all records have been processed
>
> *read and process records*
>   read a record from the file
>   *process the record*

However, with this strategy we run into problems when we reach the end of the sequential file. As our repetition construct (**perform**...**until**) is a leading decision structure, when the "read a record from the file" component indicates that the end of the file has been encountered and no further record can be read, we will attempt to process the absent record before we exit from the loop.

We could simply rewrite the *read and process records* component thus:

> *read and process records*
>   read a record from the file
>   **if** end of file has not been reached
>   **then**
>   *process the record*
>   **endif**

A preferable solution is to ensure that the exit test for the repetition structure occurs immediately after the read request. This can be achieved quite simply by adopting a technique known as "read ahead" to process records from the file. The first record from the file should now be read immediately and subsequent records should be read as soon as the previous record has been processed completely. This ensures that at any time the record that has just been read will not be processed until the next iteration of **perform...until**. The structure of many simple file processing application programs will now follow the pattern:

process file
   initialization
   perform *process each record*
      until all records have been processed
   termination

initialization
   .
   .
   .
   read first record from file

process each record
   .
   .(application dependent processing of record)
   .
   read next record from the file

termination
   .
   .
   .

There are several advantages to adopting this approach. The end of file condition is now conveniently recognized and dealt with. Also, the "special case" where we encounter an empty file can be easily identified by the initial or priming read. The arrangement of reading ahead allows the program to look ahead and examine the next record to be processed. Leading decision structures, iteration (**perform...until**), or selection (**if, case**), may then be used to determine how this record is to be processed. Depending on the logical structure of the records in the file and the particular application it will sometimes be necessary to adopt a multiple "read-ahead" technique. Read-ahead will be consistently used in this text when processing sequentially organized files.

We now return to the design of the report program.

3.5   THE PROGRAM DESIGN

If we adopt the read-ahead technique to process records from the sales file, the *initialization* component will carry out the priming or initial read from the file. If a null or empty file is discovered no area or territory summaries can be generated. A revision of the current design is in order:

> *produce sales summary report*
>   *initialization*
>   **if not** end of sales file reached
>   **then**
>   *extract summary information*
>   *print territory summary*
>   **else**
>   print "empty sales file encountered"
>   **endif**
>   *termination*
>
> *initialization*
>   .
>   .
>   .
>   read a sales record

We are now faced with another common data processing problem: the production of a report where summary information is to be produced at various levels of detail. In this case we are to produce sales totals at the salesperson, area, territory and overall levels. In addition the report is to be organized into salesperson summaries by area together with a final report detailing sales totals by territory.

One way of tackling the design of the component *extract summary information* is to organize the functions to be implemented around the processing of a single sales record from the file. What functions are involved in processing each record? A little thought will soon reveal that the processing required is dependent on whether the sales record refers to the same salesperson, area or territory as the previous sales record processed. A change in the value of any of these fields from one record to the next is called a "control break" on that field. A final control break will be generated when the final record from the file has been processed.

> *extract summary information*
>   **perform** *process each sales record*
>   **until** all sales records have been processed
>   *process final control break*

For each input record, the sales details will be added to cumulative totals for the current salesperson, area, territory and the company. First, however, we must check that no control break has occurred. We need to check for breaks on the field salesperson, area and territory. Should we check for them in any particular order? Yes, since a break on territory always implies an area break which in turn always implies a salesperson break, the checks are best made in the order territory, area, salesperson. Note also that the final control break will trigger territory, area and salesperson breaks.

> *process each sales record*
>   **if** territory **not** = previous territory
>   **then**
>   *process a territory break*
>   **else if** area **not** = previous area
>   **then**
>   *process an area break*
>   **else if** salesperson **not** = previous salesperson
>   **then**
>   *process a salesperson break*
>   **endif**
>   **endif**
>   **endif**
>   add sales amount to all cumulative totals
>   read a sales record

The refinement of *process each sales record* has identified many of the functions which are to be performed by initialization. This component will carry out the initial priming read from the file and then, providing we have not encountered an empty file, the previous territory, area and salesperson values will be initialized to the corresponding values from the first record. This ensures that this record, which has no predecessor, does not cause a control break. Also, the cumulative totals will be initialized and a heading for the initial area summary report output.

> *initialization*
>   open files
>   read a sales record
>   **if not** end of sales file reached
>   **then**
>   initialize previous territory, area and salesperson
>   set grand, territory, area and salesperson totals to zero
>   *print area summary headings*
>   **endif**

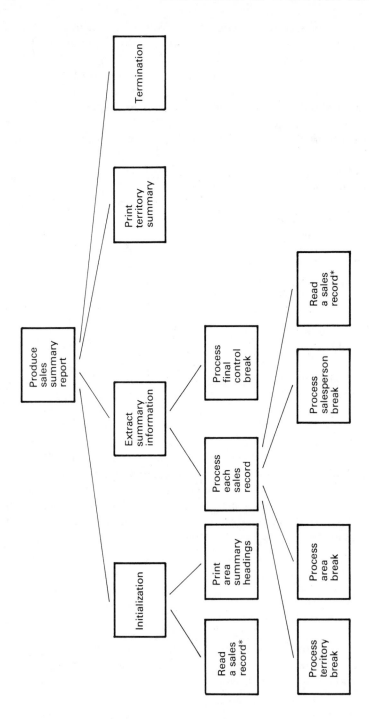

Fig. 3.1 A structure chart for the report program.

The development of the design seems to be evolving satisfactorily. However, the inexperienced designer will often wonder whether there may be some better approach which he or she has failed to discover. This may be the case and we should always search for alternative approaches to the solution of a problem. Apart from the possibility of alternatives, we may also be apprehensive about the validity of the current design. The current design is documented by the pseudocode and structure chart in Fig. 3.1.

produce sales summary report
    intialization
    if not end of sales file reached
    then
        extract summary information
        print territory summary
    else
        print "empty file encountered"
    endif
    termination

initialization
    open files
    read a sales record
    if not end of sales file reached
    then
        initialize previous territory, area and salesperson
        zero grand, territory, area and salesperson totals
        print area summary headings
    endif

extract summary information
    perform *process each sales record*
        until all sales records have been processed
    process final control break

termination
    close files

process each sales record
    if territory **not** = previous territory
    then
        process a territory break
    else if area **not** = previous area
        then
        process an area break

```
      else if salesperson not = previous salesperson
          then
              process a salesperson break
          endif
          endif
      endif
      add sales amount to all cumulative totals
      read a sales record
```

As with pseudocode, there is no accepted standard for the layout of structure charts. We will adopt the following conventions:

The subcomponents of any component in the chart are listed left to right in the same order as they appear lexically within the pseudocode elaboration of the component. The left to right ordering is merely a sensible convention. It will often, but not always, be true that this will also be the order of execution of the components in the chart. The order of execution will be different in the case of components which are conditionally executed.

Special provision must be made for components which are subcomponents of more than one component. These may be handled by using a single box to represent the common component. However, this may make it impossible to draw the chart without lines crossing and also means that we no longer have a tree structure as components do not now have unique predecessors. We will adopt the convention of repeating components each time they are used in the chart but identifying them as duplicate components in some way. For example, by using an asterisk as shown in Fig. 3.1 to identify the "read a sales record" components.

What steps can be taken to reassure ourselves, or otherwise, as to the validity of the evolving design?

(a) Perform a "walkthrough" of the design and validate its correctness in terms of the abstract statements at each level of the design.

(b) Assess whether the design is simple and easy to understand or overly complex.

(c) Assess whether each component of the design performs an individual function or whether some functions are split between two or more components.

(d) Examine the structure chart. Do any of the components have more than, say, five subcomponents? A component with a high "fan-out" or large span of control is a warning signal of a possibly poor design. It may indicate that the component is over complex in the sense that it controls too many subcomponents. A possible solution may be to define intermediate levels in the chart.

In our case, all the signs are positive and we can proceed with some measure of confidence. You will have noticed that the design has not evolved on a strict level-by-level basis. In practice, it will often be necessary to pursue the design of some critical component for a few levels to establish the suitability of the design approach. However, we should endeavor to keep as close to a strict top-down approach as possible. Examination of the structure chart suggests that we should now study the refinement of the component *print territory summary*.

This component will produce a summary of sales by territory and a grand total monthly sales figure for the company. The information for the territory summary will have been gathered during the processing of the sales detail records from the file. How is this information to be represented? The obvious choice is to build a table whose entries will associate a territory with its monthly sales, and which can then be examined to produce the territory summary report. The specification informs us that currently the company has 12 territories but that expansion is anticipated. The table must be implemented in a way which ensures that an increase in the number of territories can be easily accommodated.

> *print territory summary*
>> *print territory summary headings*
>> **perform** *print sales summary for each territory*
>>> **until** all territory summaries are printed
>> *print grand sales total*

The final control break encountered when the end of file is reached will cause a break on territory, area and salesperson. In our example, no functions particular to only the final control break are required and the component *process final control break* can be achieved by invoking *process territory break*.

> *process final control break*
>> *process territory break*

This pseudocode may seem redundant; *process final control break* is synonymous with *process territory break*. As our program specification stands at the moment this is true but we should always be programming for change, anticipating inevitable future modifications that will be asked for. It is therefore desirable to keep the processing of the final control break an independent component. Should a modification arise associated with the final control break, for example, a message to indicate the end of the area summary reports, the modification can be accommodated more easily.

A control break on the territory field will be handled by first invoking the component to process an area break and then dealing with functions specific to the territory break, i.e. enter the accumulated territory total into the territory sales summary table and reset the values of territory and territory total.

>*process territory break*
>   *process an area break*
>   enter territory total into territory table
>   reset previous territory code
>   reset territory total to zero

The components to process area and salesperson breaks can be refined in a similar fashion to the territory break component. Both of these components will also cause area summary information to be output.

>*process an area break*
>   *process a salesperson break*
>   *process end of area summary*
>   reset previous area code
>   reset area total to 0

>*process a salesperson break*
>   format salesperson summary line
>   *print area summary report line*
>   reset previous salesperson number and name
>   reset salesperson total to 0

The only components remaining for refinement relate to the output of the summary information. Their design is largely straightforward except for the fact that we adopt the strategy of channeling the actual printing of report body lines for each summary through a single design component. Once again, the motivation for this is one of designing the program in such a way that modification will not cause major design upheavals.

For example, a modification suggested in the exercises at the end of this chapter requires that both summary reports be amended to include logic to handle the possibility of page overflow on a summary report. Such a requirement can be met more easily if the change impacts only a single design component rather than many. We need to produce designs in such a way that changes have only a localized effect.

The final program design language algorithm for the report program, including the refinement of the summary output components, is shown opposite:

produce sales summary report
   initialization
  if not end of sales file reached
  then
    extract summary information
    print territory summary
  else
    print "empty file encountered"
  endif
  termination

initialization
  open files
  read first sales record
  if not end of sales file reached
  then
    initialize previous territory, area and salesperson
    zero grand, territory, area and salesperson totals
    initialize territory table
    set page count to 1
    print area summary headings
  endif

extract summary information
  perform process each sales record
    until all sales records have been processed
  process final control break

print territory summary
  print territory summary headings
  perform *print sales summary for each territory*
    until all territory summaries are printed
  print grand sales total

termination
  close files

process each sales record
  if territory **not** = previous territory
  then
    process a territory break
  else if area **not** = previous area
    then
      process an area break

else if salesperson **not** = previous salesperson
　　then
　　　　process a salesperson break
　　endif
　　endif
endif
add sales amount to all cumulative totals
read next sales record

process final control break
　process territory break

process territory break
　process an area break
　enter territory total into territory table
　reset previous territory code
　reset territory total to zero

process an area break
　process a salesperson break
　process end of area summary
　reset previous area code
　reset area total to 0

process end of area summary
　format area total line
　print area summary report line
　if all sales records have not been processed
　then
　　print area summary headings
　endif

process a salesperson break
　format salesperson summary line
　print area summary report line
　reset previous salesperson number and name
　reset salesperson total to 0

print area summary headings
　print report headings
　output area heading summary lines

print area summary report line
　output area summary line

print territory summary headings
   print report headings
   print territory summary heading lines

print sales summary for each territory
   format next territory summary line
   print territory summary report line

print grand total line
   format grand total line
   print territory summary report line

print territory summary report line
   print territory summary line

print report headings
   output report heading lines
   add 1 to page count

3.6   AN ALTERNATIVE DESIGN

The design we have presented was based on the notion of designing the program around the processing of a single sales record, *viz.*:

extract summary information
   perform *process each sales record*
     until all sales records have been processed
   process final control break

process each sales record
   if territory **not** = previous territory
   then
     process a territory break
   else if area **not** = previous area
     then
       process an area break
     else if salesperson **not** = previous salesperson
       then
         process a salesperson break
       endif
     endif
   endif
   add sales amount to all cumulative totals
   read a sales record

This strategy seemed to work out quite well but there may well be equally acceptable or even better designs which remain to be discovered. An alternative strategy would be to bind the design more closely to the structure of the input file. That is, think of the sales file as being made up of groups of territory records, with each territory composed of groups of area records etc. This would lead to the following outline structure:

> *extract summary information*
> > **perform** *process territory groups*
> > > **until** all sales records have been processed
> > *process final control break*
>
> *process territory groups*
> > **perform** *process area groups*
> > > **until** territory **not** = previous territory **or**
> > > all sales records have been processed
> > *process a territory break*
>
> *process area groups*
> > **perform** *process salesperson groups*
> > > **until** area **not** = previous area **or**
> > > all sales records have been processed
> > *process an area break*
>
> *process salesperson groups*
> > **perform** *process each sales record*
> > > **until** salesperson **not** = previous salesperson **or**
> > > all sales records have been processed
> > *process a salesperson break*
>
> *process each sales record*
> > .
> > .
> > .
> read a sales record

Notice that the control break components now only perform functions specific to a particular break. For example, *process a territory break* no longer invokes the area break component as this break has already been processed prior to recognition of that of the territory break.

The evaluation of different design alternatives is most often a very difficult task. We can, however, use the following design attributes for comparison purposes: complexity, ease of understanding, correctness, modifiability and maintainability.

In our example, there is little to choose between the two alternatives. The original was most influenced by the functions the program was to carry out while the alternative was more influenced by the structure of the data being manipulated. Although these alternatives are visually quite different, closer examination shows that logically they are extremely similar.

3.7 SUMMARY

In this chapter we have seen the Top-down Stepwise Refinement method successfully applied to the design of a typical business data processing problem. Several important aspects of the program design activity have been emphasized.

(a) Top-down design does not proceed on a strict level-by-level basis. It is often necessary to explore the design of key components through several levels of refinement before making a decision to adopt or reject a design approach.

(b) Almost always there is more than one solution to a problem. Search for alternatives.

(c) Ensure, as far as possible, the correctness of the design at each level of refinement.

(d) Programs must be designed in the knowledge that they will almost certainly require significant maintenance and modification in the future. This will necessarily impact on many of the decisions taken during the design of a program. It may be necessary, for example, to ensure that design components are functionally independent.

Also, two important program design techniques have been introduced:

(a) Read-ahead, a technique for processing records from a sequential file has been presented. In the simplest of cases, the first record from the file should be read immediately and subsequent records should be read as soon as the previous record has been processed completely. In some cases, it will be necessary to read more than one record ahead.

(b) The control break logic used when summary information is to be extracted from sequentially organized files at various levels of detail.

3.8 EXERCISES

1. Our original program specification necessarily omitted some features normally found in typical real-life report program examples. Amend the program design solution presented in the chapter to accommodate the following specification changes:

    (a) Sequence checking of the input sales file is now required. That is, verify that the sales records are ordered by salesperson number within area within territory. The program should abort on finding a sequence error.

    (b) In addition to the summaries produced by the original program, a summary of sales by area for each territory is to be printed as shown below. You may assume that there will be a maximum of 10 areas per territory.

NU-WAVE COSMETICS

MONTHLY SALES SUMMARY REPORT   PAGE 10

TERRITORY 09

AREA	SALES ($)
1	3359.34
3	5378.99
7	5996.54
.	.
.	.
.	.
.	.

TOTAL MONTHLY SALES $32741.39

This summary should be printed on a territory break.

    (c) Page overflow is to be recognized on any summary. In such circumstances the summary should be continued after a page throw and generation of appropriate header information.

    (d) The input sales file contains a trailer record (a record appended to the end of the file), containing a total of the individual monetary amounts held on the file. This amount should be checked against the accumulated total generated within the program and suitable information output if the two totals disagree.

2. Consider the impact on the program design solution presented in the chapter if the following specification changes were required.

    (a) It is possible for a salesperson to appear in more than one area. Note that the original program specification made no mention of this possibility or how it should be handled.

    (b) The number of territories into which the sales function of the company is divided was increased by a factor of ten. *Hint*: would it help if we relaxed the requirement that a single output file should be used to produce the sales summary report?

4

Guidelines for the Design Process

4.1 INTRODUCTION

Top-down decomposition of an algorithm is not an automatic straight-forward activity that can be done without thought. There are no set rules or procedures which if followed will lead to clear, understandable, correct and efficient programs. On the contrary, program design is difficult and it involves inspiration, creativity and design decision-making.

Unless we intend relying heavily on inspiration we need additional help. This chapter describes various guidelines that have been formulated in recent years to aid the design process. We discuss:

component size
complexity
searching for alternative solutions
correctness
ignoring detail
the order of decomposition
data hiding
coupling and cohesion
shared components
program performance

The motivations behind using guidelines are the same as those for structured programming:

51

ease of construction
reliability
ease of maintenance
meeting performance requirements

The trouble is that sometimes these goals conflict with each other. For example, it often takes longer to write a program that executes more quickly. So normally we have to trade-off one objective against another and make a balanced judgement based on individual circumstances. Nowadays, however, computer hardware is becoming ever cheaper, so saving the time of the programmer is becoming of increasing importance. Generally, therefore, we take the view that program performance is of secondary importance compared with the other goals. Thus, during the design process issues like clarity and simplicity should take precedence over efficiency. We continue this discussion in Section 4.11 on Program Performance.

Many of the guidelines we discuss are about the issue of how to split a program into constituent parts that display certain desirable properties. COBOL provides three ways of splitting a program into parts—paragraphs, sections and subprograms. Each has its own strengths and weaknesses. In this chapter we refer to any of these programming elements as a component. We also use the term to refer to a sequence of pseudocode statements.

4.2   COMPONENT SIZE

At each stage in decomposing an algorithm we are faced with the question, "how much detail should we consider at this stage?" or, "into how many steps should we break down this step?" For example, in developing a program that scans a file to produce a report (see Chapter 3), should we start with:

initialize
generate report
terminate

or should we write down a more detailed algorithm at this stage:

initialize
perform *process a record*
   until end of file
print report totals
terminate

or even:

```
open files
print headings
set totals to zero
read first record
perform process a record
   until end of file
print total 1
print total 2
close files
stop
```

The same problem arises at each and every stage of the expansion.

This question about the size of a component has been considered a great deal in the past and particularly during the phase when "modular programming" was in vogue. There are two points of view:

(a) A component should occupy no more than a page (about 40 to 50 lines).

(b) A component should normally take up about seven lines or less, and in no circumstances more than nine.

The first suggestion takes account of the difficulty in understanding logic that spills over from one page to another.

Those who argue for the "magic number" seven do so on the basis of experimental results from psychology. Research indicates that the human brain is capable of comprehending only about seven things at once. This does not mean that we can remember only seven things; clearly we can remember many more, but we can only retain in short-term memory and study as a complete, related set of objects, a few things. The number of objects ranges from about five to nine, depending on the individual and the objects under study. The implication is that if we wish to understand completely a piece of program or a piece of pseudocode it should only be of this length.

Our own personal experience endorses this suggestion; we have tried it and it works. It also fits in very well with the paragraph facility of COBOL. Because of the nature of COBOL, paragraphs do tend to be short—in general consisting of 10 rather than 100 statements. So the authors recommend, as a guideline, that we break down an item into about seven or less pseudocode statements. The resulting COBOL program should have paragraphs with the same number of statements. You will see that in the examples given in this book we tend to do this. Please do not feel that we wish to be rigid and dogmatic about this; if you feel that your solution to a problem breaks down naturally into ten statements and anything less will distort your idea, then we would not wish to stand in your way, but we would argue that usually it is easy to honor this guideline.

A final point. Component size is related to complexity. We would argue that the algorithm:

> **if** stock on hand < reorder level
> **then** *print exception line*
> **else**
>   *print normal line*
> **endif**

is more complicated to understand than:

> *check stock level*
> *print report line* 1
> *print report line* 2

even though each consists of essentially three pseudocode statements. We suggest therefore, in cases where the logic consists of something other than a sequential list of steps, that there should be even fewer than seven steps.

An objection to the idea of having only a few statements goes like this. By having a few statements we are only increasing the number of levels, so all we are doing is to decrease complexity in one way (the number of statements) at the cost of increased complexity in another way (the number of levels). So we gain nothing overall. Expressed graphically, either we have a short fat tree or a tall thin tree. Either way the tree has just as many branches; it is just as complex, but in having small components we create many, and we attract the criticism of having devised confusingly bitty structures.

It appears to the authors that the error in this argument is this. Either when developing or when reading a structured program we do not look at the whole program at once. Instead, we focus attention on only a single component at a time; we study the logic of that one component in isolation. When we do so, we comprehend what each of the constituent steps does from its statement as an English sentence. When we have completed an examination of one component in its entirety we turn our attention to another. At no time do we need to comprehend two or more program components at the same time. So it is the complexity of individual components that matters.

Others who argue against small components point out that they give rise to slower programs because of the increased overhead of subroutine linkage. But nowadays a programmer's time can cost significantly more than a computer's time. The question here is whether it is more important for a program to be easy to understand or whether it is more important for it to run quickly. These requirements may well conflict and only individual circumstances can resolve the issue. It may well be better, however, first to design, code and test a program using the guideline of small components. Then, if performance is important, particular COBOL paragraphs that are invoked frequently can be rewritten in the bodies of those paragraphs that use them. We discuss the issue of performance more fully in Section 4.11.

4.3 COMPLEXITY

In the early days of programming, particularly when resources like main store and c.p.u. acted as stringent constraints, it was considered usual to try hard to make programs efficient. One effect of this was that programmers were given every encouragement to use sophisticated or contorted ideas. Nowadays the situation is rather different—the pressure is on to reduce the development time of programs and ease the burden of maintenance. So the emphasis is on writing programs that are clear and simple, and therefore easy to check, understand and modify.

Some programmers regard this as a threat; they fear that if they attempt to simplify their programs they will be ignoring the skills that they have accumulated over the years, and that their programs will be in some sense inferior products. There are several responses to this: first, searching and finding a simple solution to a problem is not easy. Second, even confining ourselves to uncomplicated solutions, there is tremendous scope for the invention and investigation of alternatives. Third, a simple program is more likely to work quickly and then go on working after it is put into service. (This cannot be bad for our esteem.) Fourth, the programmer who (inevitably) has to locate the bug in our program or else modify it to meet a changed specification will respect us and thank us the more if our design is easy to follow rather than riddled with clever but incomprehensible tricks.

If we look at the world of design engineering we see that a good engineer insists on maintaining a complete understanding and control over every aspect of the project. The more difficult the project the more firmly the insistence on simplicity— without it no-one can understand what is going on. Often programmers exhibit the exact opposite characteristic; they deliberately avoid simple solutions and gain satisfaction from the complexities of their designs. Perhaps we should try to emulate the approach of the engineers.

But what is meant by simple? We mean that components are small in the sense described above. We mean that data items are only used for a single purpose, not for different reasons at different times. We mean that the program does not modify itself as it executes, in the way that some COBOL features allow. We mean any aspect of the program that does not appear completely clear to an inexperienced programmer. We reiterate that it may well take a long time to devise such a program.

We firmly ignore the issue of program performance for the present, postponing it until Section 4.11.

4.4   SEARCHING FOR ALTERNATIVE SOLUTIONS

There is always more than one solution to a problem, more than one design that meets the specification. We suggest that it should be our aim not just to find a single solution, but to find one that best meets the design objectives.

The use of structured programming provides a good framework for the investigation of alternative designs. If a design seems over-complex, or in some other way unsatisfactory, we can retrace our design, level by level, considering alternatives at each level. It will often be desirable to replace whole subtrees using this process. We should not be afraid to explore possibilities through several levels of refinement before making a decision to adopt or reject them.

The use of a program design language means that alternative designs can be written down quite quickly. More important, the process is completely under control—we know precisely which component of the program we are investigating and what its relationship is to the rest of the program.

4.5   CORRECTNESS

There is an increasingly strong school of thought that insists that a program should be accompanied by a rigorous mathematical proof that it meets its specification. Although such proofs are, in principle, desirable it is far from clear whether proving a program is a practical proposition given the present state of the art. Whether or not proving is feasible for program code, an algorithm written in pseudocode cannot be subject to proof because of the informality of the English sentences it contains. The authors' view is that proving will never be seriously adopted for applications programming.

What can be done, however, is to carefully check the algorithm at each level of decomposition. Have all the right steps been included? Are they in the right order? The fact that each component has one entry point (at the beginning) and a single exit (at the end) considerably aids this process of checking. Writing down only a small number of statements within each component also helps. This kind of informal checking for correctness is invaluable.

4.6 IGNORING DETAIL

At any stage of decomposition it is well worth trying to ignore the detail of lower levels. Do not worry about how lower levels will work but concentrate on the correctness of the current level. Express the current level in terms of black boxes each of which perform some clear function. The question of how the interior of the black boxes is to be designed is postponed until the present level is complete.

This is all easier said than done, and it is difficult to prevent ourselves from thinking about other components, whether or not we think we know how to design them.

The real test of whether we have truly accepted that program design is worthwhile is that we exercise restraint at each stage of design. In particular we must resist the temptation to rush on to the coding stage.

4.7 THE ORDER OF DECOMPOSITION

Given the pseudocode of a component of program, like:

initialize
perform *process record*
    until end of file
print totals
terminate

which statement should we tackle first in trying to break down the solution? There are several possibilities:

(a)   Start with the first and break down the components one by one, in the order that they are written down. This will avoid something being missed out.

(b)   Since it does not matter which statement is broken down first, choose any one that you like.

(c)   Choose whichever seems to be the simplest statement, presumably *initialize* or *terminate* in the above example. The success of dealing with it will create confidence, and it may give insights into the more complex part of the algorithm.

(d)   Choose whichever seems to be the most complicated statement—presumably *process record* in the above example.

Note that options (a) and (b) presume that the different statements within an algorithm are largely independent of one another. Generally this is a fallacy. The statements should be functionally independent, that is they should do completely separate things, but often they will operate upon common data, that is, they will be data interdependent.

Option (d) is generally regarded as the best strategy because by exposing the detail of the largest component light will be shed on the requirements of the others.

4.8   DATA HIDING

Data hiding, information hiding or encapsulation as it is sometimes called, is a way of structuring a system or a program. It suggests that for each data structure (or file structure), all of the following should be contained in a single module:

(a)   the structure itself
(b)   the statements that access the structure
(c)   the statements that modify the structure.

The idea is to meet three aims:

(a)   *Changeability*. If various design decisions are changed, such as a file structure, changes should be confined to as few program components as possible (preferably one).
(b)   *Independent development*. When a system is being implemented by a team of programmers, the interfaces between the components should be as simple as possible. The suggestion is that the interfaces should, therefore, be by means of calls on subprograms rather than by means of access to shared data and file structures.
(c)   *Comprehensibility*. For the purposes of design, checking, testing and maintenance it should be possible to understand individual components independently of others. Suppose, however, that two components, A and B, communicate via shared data or files. The shared information structure may well contain elements that A alone uses in order to access it. To understand component B it is necessary to understand the shared information structure, and this in turn necessitates knowing about the additional pieces of data that A uses. So in studying B it turns out that we have to understand something of how A works. Thus it is difficult to understand the components in isolation. By contrast, data hiding tends to enforce clearer separation between components.

Chapter 11 shows an example of a COBOL program structured according to the principle of data hiding. There the problem requires that information is held in a file or a data structure. The program is required to accept and respond to commands from a terminal. The two parts of the program are separated (as much as COBOL allows), so that the part of the program that analyses commands knows nothing of the workings of the part that accesses the data.

The subprogram feature of COBOL provides one way in which data hiding can be assisted by the language. All data in a COBOL subprogram are inaccessible to any other subprogram (unless explicitly communicated in a parameter list). Unfortunately a COBOL subprogram cannot have two or more entry points. So the way to use a subprogram to implement data hiding is as follows. Group the required operations in the subprogram together with the data or files that they act upon. Use a parameter of the call (for example a number) to identify the particular operation required. Code a switch at the start of the subprogram to test the value of the parameter and accordingly invoke the appropriate piece of code.

For example, suppose that we have to write a text formatting program. Suppose also that we find it necessary to assemble a line to be printed by placing in it characters, one by one, until the line is full. We could construct a COBOL subprogram that has the three functions:

(a)   Empty the line (it is the start of the processing)
(b)   Place one character in the line. If the line is full, print it
(c)   (There are no more characters.) Print the remaining line (which is probably unfilled).

We could specify that the way the subprogram is used is by coding:

CALL "PRINT" USING FUNCTION-NUMBER, CHARACTER.

where FUNCTION-NUMBER is 1, 2, or 3 corresponding to each of the above functions. In the case of the second function, CHARACTER communicates the character to be output. Now we have a situation where all information about the output line is hidden within the subprogram. The record itself, its length and the subscript that moves along it are invisible and inaccessible from outside the subprogram. No unintentional change can be made to them. Every operation on these data items is localized within the subprogram. For this reason the actions can be more easily designed and checked.

In summary, the principle of data hiding means that, at the end of the design process, any data structure or file is accessed only via certain well-defined, specific paragraphs, sections or subprograms.

4.9   COUPLING AND COHESION

The ideas of coupling and cohesion are guidelines for splitting a program into components, termed "modules", in a desirable way. The essence of the approach is that a program should be divided into modules in such a way that there is a minimum of interaction between modules (low coupling) and, conversely, a high degree of interaction within a module (high cohesion). If this can be achieved, then an individual module can be designed, coded, tested or amended without the complications of having to deal with other modules.

First let us consider coupling. Suppose we are amending a COBOL program and have decided that a change to one particular paragraph is necessary. When we change the paragraph we can easily see any change in the relationships of control between this and the other paragraphs by looking at the PERFORM statements. We can also see what changes in access to data have been made. But we may be faced with some uncertainty in analyzing secondary effects of changing access to data. For example, suppose that in the DATA DIVISION there is a table and a number that subscripts it. Suppose that, in the paragraph we are altering, we reverse the order of the two operations of incrementing the subscript and accessing an item in the table. To sort out the implications of this change for other paragraphs that access the subscript may well be difficult. We have a situation where the coupling between paragraphs is stronger than we would like; the effects of a change to one paragraph may disrupt others. So COBOL paragraphs, all sharing access to a single DATA DIVISION are potentially strongly coupled to each other.

If a COBOL program has been constructed as a set of subprograms, then the coupling between the subprograms is weaker than if the same pieces of program had been written as paragraphs within the same subprogram. The data that appears in any one subprogram is inaccessible to other subprograms, so that there is no coupling by this route. Interactions are limited to explicit call statements between subprograms. If no parameters are used in these calls then the amount of coupling is virtually none. On the other hand, a subprogram could pass its complete DATA DIVISION as parameters, thus intensifying the coupling. Judicious design should therefore minimize parameter passing between subprograms (thereby reducing coupling).

On the issue of cohesion, a scheme is presented for classifying the various types of interaction that can occur within a module. These range from low cohesion (undesirable) at the top of the list, to high cohesion (desirable) at the bottom of the list:

(a)   coincidental cohesion, in which the components are in the module purely by coincidence

(b)   logical cohesion, in which the module performs a set of independent but logically similar functions, for example, a set of different output routines

(c) temporal cohesion, in which the module performs a set of functions that are related in time, for example, a set of initialization operations

(d) procedural cohesion, in which the operations in the module correspond to a grouping of an arbitrary number of sequential operations

(e) communicational cohesion, in which functions acting on common data are grouped together

(f) sequential cohesion, in which the operations in a module collaborate in modifying a piece of data. Typically such a module accepts data from one module, modifies it, and passes it on to another module

(g) functional cohesion, in which every operation in the module contributes towards the performance of a single well-defined task.

Note that there is a strong correspondence between "communicational cohesion" listed in this scheme and the idea of "data hiding" described in Section 4.8.

How is this scheme of grades of cohesion related to functional decomposition? Fortunately the top-down stepwise-refinement method of program design presented in this book tends to lead automatically to functionally bound modules. This is because the technique consistently concentrates on *what* the program is to do—the functional approach to design. So modules with the favoured functional cohesion are presented at every stage of design.

There are, however, exceptions. Sometimes components with temporal (poor), procedural (better), or sequential (acceptable) cohesion arise from a functional approach. The suggested way of avoiding them is to apply some rudimentary literary analysis. We are asked to examine the statement of the function of the component under consideration. It should only have one verb and a single object that is acted upon by the verb. If on the other hand several verbs appear, we should beware of procedural cohesion. Again, if terms like initialize are mentioned, then temporal cohesion may be present. Sometimes, however, especially if we have no choice, we have to settle for a form of cohesion less desirable than the best.

4.10 SHARED COMPONENTS

Experienced programmers are used to the idea of designing subprograms that can be used in a variety of situations, thus saving both effort and main store. How does this fit in with the ideas of structured programming? Michael Jackson argues as follows. Suppose that during functional decomposition we arrive at a structure in which a lower level component appears as part of two or more higher level components. Expressed in terms of a tree this corresponds to a leaf growing from two or more branches. Two questions arise: first, how was the component designed? The method prescribes that a component arises from the decomposition of another. If a component is shared, from which one of its mothers did it emerge? Surely you can't design two things at the same time. So the shared component must be unsatisfactory; it can't be completely suitable in more than one context. The second problem concerns testing and debugging. If a fault occurs in a shared component it is not clear how it was called or performed—it might have been along any of a number of branches. So location and correction of the fault is made more difficult.

Because of these problems, Jackson argues that if any shared components are to be employed then they should arise only from the following, bottom-up methodology. When first thinking about the solution to a problem ideas arise in the mind. For example, in a particular program, perhaps the use of tables strongly suggests itself. However, although COBOL supports the idea of tables it falls short of providing ready made facilities to add, subtract, multiply and compare tables. Why not augment COBOL's facilities and implement a set of general-purpose table manipulation routines? This would make COBOL more suitable for solving the immediate problem, and the routines might well come in useful in the future. We see that the design of these routines has not emerged from a strictly top-down approach, but from bottom-up considerations—starting with COBOL and trying to make it more convenient.

The specification of what shareable, general-purpose subprograms do and how they are used should be completely independent of any particular context in which the routines might be used. The same should be true of how the routines work, and of the testing they are subjected to. Such routines should be placed in a common system library.

4.11 PROGRAM PERFORMANCE

Before we discuss how to consider efficiency in the design process, we pose the question: is efficiency what we really want? Or are we really more interested in reliability, ease of maintenance, or meeting project deadlines? These days main store and processors are relatively cheap compared with the cost of constuction of programs. Priorities have changed since the days of trying to squeeze a program into the small memory available, but there are, of course, many applications like on-line systems where fast response is essential. Similarly, there are still machines without virtual memory, where main store may be at a premium.

Even in situations where efficiency is deemed to be important, it is vital to analyse carefully what the requirements are. Amongst the possibilities are:

small store occupancy
low c.p.u. usage
fast run-time
small file size.

Usually these objectives are mutually contradictory. For example in a program to calculate tax it is quicker to look up the tax in a table in main store than to calculate it each time it is required. But the program with the table is much larger. As another example, a program with repetitive code written out in full is longer but faster than the same program written with a loop. Thus high run-time speed and small main store usage are often contradictory. So if efficiency is an issue, let us make sure we agree precisely what we mean in each specific situation.

Another problem with optimizing a program is that by the time we are given a program to write, decisions have already been taken at the system design stage that significantly affect the performance of the system and often preclude any worthwhile efforts by the programmer. For example, file design (with immediate implications for access method) is normally carried out before program design and in a data processing application this will largely determine the performance of the system.

There are several other elements of the environment of a program that can radically affect performance:

(a) Choice of the representation of information in a file. Usually there is the possibility of packing the data, giving a small file but a c.p.u. overhead in performing data conversions.
(b) Choice of file block-size. A large block-size may mean fewer disk head movements but larger main store buffers.
(c) The decision about the number of input–output buffers. Again, in general, the more buffers the faster the processing but the greater the main store utilization.
(d) In an on-line system queue lengths play the same role as the number of buffers do in batch systems.

One easy way of tuning is to invoke an optimizing compiler. It has the virtue of leaving the program structure intact.

If we have to consider the performance of a particular program, there are two approaches that we can adopt. One strategy is to take into account performance requirements throughout the design process. We can adopt an idea and tentatively pursue its decomposition until we realize the consequences. We can similarly develop other possibilities and then choose between them. Thus the method of functional decomposition provides a framework for investigating alternative designs.

The other approach to improving the performance of a program is as follows. First design, code and test the program with clarity, simplicity, generality and good modularity as goals. Then assess which parts of the program contribute significantly to slow run-time or large store occupancy or whatever the requirement is. Studies suggest that normally it is only small parts of a program that dictate its performance. So it may only be necessarry to recode small parts of the program, leaving the overall design intact. But, if necessary, transform the (clear) structure into the structure with the desired performance, fully documenting the act of mutilation.

4.12 SUMMARY

In this chapter we have discussed a whole range of considerations that should be taken into account during the structured design of a program. The aims of the design process are:

(a)   ease of construction
(b)   reliability
(c)   ease of maintenance
(d)   meeting program performance targets.

These guidelines help us in three ways:

(a)   they tell us what to do during the act of decomposition
(b)   they try to lead us to programs that are clear, simple and flexible
(c)   they remind us of the role of program performance.

To an inexperienced programmer the list of considerations may seem formidable, but programming by any methodology is not easy: it involves the continual exercise of creativity and judgement, enhanced by experience. The authors hope that the reader will appreciate that many of the ideas of software engineering are in their infancy. There is at this time no complete methodology that tells us in detail how to design a program.

4.13 FURTHER READING

1.   Parnas, D. L., "On the Criteria to be Used in Decomposing Systems into Modules", *Comm. ACM*, **15** (12), pp.1053–1058, 1972.
     This paper introduced the idea of data hiding.

2. Yourdon, E. and Constantine, L. L., *Structured Design*, Prentice-Hall, Englewood Cliffs, N.J., 1979.
The ideas of coupling and cohesion are discussed at length in this book. There is also treatment of the issue of the optimal size of a module.

3. Shneiderman, B., *Software Psychology*, Winthrop, Cambridge, Mass., 1981.
The individual psychology of programmers and how it relates to the complexity of programs is described.

4. Jackson, M. A., *Principles of Program Design*, Academic Press, London, 1975.
The issue of shared components is discussed.

5

Design of a Validate Program

5.1 INTRODUCTION

In this chapter we follow the steps involved in the design of a specific program. The primary aim is to show how, using the structured methodology, alternative designs can be developed and a good design arrived at. In Chapter 3 two good designs were developed in a fairly straightforward fashion. By contrast, in this chapter, we chart the progress of the search for a good design by means of a series of attempts. It turns out that this particular program can be fairly complex and, since run-time speed and main store size are not issues, the criterion for a successful solution is that the program not only works but is simple—easy to check and maintain.

A second aim of this chapter is to present a typical solution for a very common type of program in data processing—a program to validate (or check) input data.

The deliberations over the structure of this program show that there is considerable scope for creativity, originality and imagination. The use of structured programming does not automatically, and without thinking, lead to a good program.

5.2 THE PROGRAM SPECIFICATION

A validate program is required for a computerized gas billing system. The program is one of a suite of batch programs that together maintain records of customers and their bills. The program is to accept as input a set of transactions punched on cards. The program is to produce as output:

(a) A listing of invalid transactions. This listing should be suitably formatted and annotated with messages indicating the nature of any errors found in each transaction. Note that a transaction may have more than one error. The program should check for and report on all errors wherever possible.

(b) A file of all valid transactions. The records of the file have the same format as the card transactions.

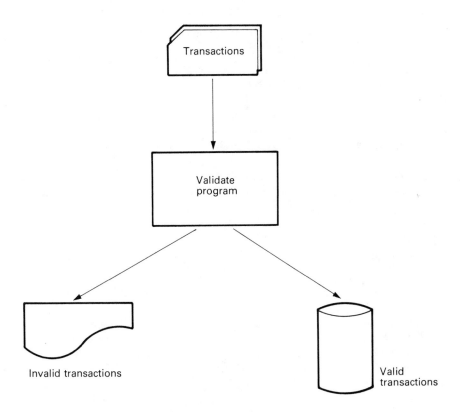

Fig. 5.1 Computer run diagram.

The program's role is illustrated by a computer run diagram shown in Fig. 5.1. Individual transactions are identified by a transaction code shown overleaf:

Transaction code	Transaction
1	meter reading
2	customer payment
3	adjustment of meter number
4	adjustment of customer name
5	delete customer record
6/7	add new customer record

Note that two cards, each with a different code, are required to describe the addition of a new customer. The input layout for each transaction type is

Table 5.1   Fields to be checked*

Field	Cols	Chars	Range/Valid content
Every transaction (types 1 to 7)			
transaction code	1	1	1–7
reference number	2–7	6	010000–020000
Meter reading (type 1)			
meter reading	8–12	5	numeric
Customer payment (type 2)			
payment amount	8–13	6	numeric, non-zero (always positive)
Adjust meter number (type 3)			
new meter number	8–13	6	numeric
Adjust name (type 4)			
adjusted name	8–27	20	non-blank
Delete customer record (type 5)			
no other fields			
New customer record 1 (type 6)			
customer name	8–27	20	non-blank
address line 1	28–47	20	non-blank
address line 2	48–67	20	non-blank
New customer record 2 (type 7)			
meter number	8–13	6	numeric
reading date	14–15	2	2–28
previous index	16–20	5	numeric
tariff	21	1	"S" or "N"
special instructions	22–36	15	
consumption	37–41	5	numeric or blank
amount due	42–47	6	numeric or blank
date	48–53	6	numeric or blank
b/f balance	54–59	6	numeric or blank

*In numeric fields, leading spaces are not valid.

shown in Table 5.1, together with the required contents of each field. In addition:

(a) Only transaction codes in the range 1 to 7 are valid. If the transaction code is invalid the remainder of the transaction is ignored.

(b) For type 7 transactions, the following relationship must hold between meter reading date and customer reference number:

last two digits of customer reference number = reading date + 10

(c) The addition of a new customer record involves a pair of transactions with codes 6 and 7. Such pairs must be in the order 6 followed by 7, immediately adjacent to each other and have the same customer reference number. The complete pair of transactions should be rejected if an error in either or both of the pair is detected.

(d) With the exception of note (c) above, there is no sequencing of the transactions.

5.3   INITIAL THOUGHTS

One way to begin dealing with this program is to make a list of all the different errors that the program should be capable of detecting. This list is given below. It may be regarded as a clarification of the specification.

    1   transaction code invalid
    2   reference number invalid
    3   meter reading invalid
    4   payment amount invalid
    5   new meter number invalid
    6   adjusted name invalid
    7   customer name invalid
    8   address invalid
    9   reference numbers different
   10   meter number invalid
   11   reading date invalid
   12   previous index invalid
   13   tariff invalid
   14   consumption invalid
   15   amount due invalid
   16   date invalid
   17   b/f balance invalid
   18   6 not followed by 7
   19   7 preceded by invalid 6

The problem of printing these error messages can be analyzed like this. More than one error may be present in an individual transaction and these errors will be detected at different points in the program. Transactions must be sent to a file if they are correct, but printed together with messages if they are erroneous. Rather than scatter throughout the program tests to see whether an erroneous transaction has been printed already, it seems preferable to set up a table, with one entry for each of the possible errors. When a transaction is input the whole table is cleared. Whenever a particular error is detected the corresponding table entry is marked. When all checks have been carried out on a particular transaction the table can be scanned and all relevant error messages printed.

This approach is an attempt to foresee and avoid unnecessary complexities in the program. It is an example of where a programmer's experience can short-cut the development process. The technique also makes the program easier to maintain in the event of changes to the program requirements.

If this technique is adopted then the program will be further simplified if a second table is set up containing the texts of the error messages. This table can be subscripted by the error number to extract the corresponding message.

5.4   FIRST DESIGN

We start the design as usual at the top level, realizing, as discussed earlier, that the initialization will involve reading the first transaction, and that the last thing to do after processing transaction is to read the next.

> *validate*
>   *initialize*
>   **perform** *check transaction*
>   **until** end of file
>   *complete processing*
>   stop

The next step is to investigate what is apparently the most complex part of the algorithm, check transaction. If types 6 and 7 transactions were completely independent we could use a **case** statement that included all seven valid transactions.

> *check transaction*
>   **case** transaction type **of**
>   1: *check type* 1

```
    2: check type 2
    3: check type 3
    4: check type 4
    5: check type 5
    6: check type 6
    7: check type 7
    else: error 1
endcase
```

This would be very natural, orderly and straightforward. But we must, in fact, check that types 6 and 7 occur together, and this leads to difficulties which make this program thought-provoking and far from trivial.

In this first design we attempt to control things by deciding that the part of the program that checks a type 6 transaction should go on to read the following transaction (which will normally be a type 7).

```
check transaction
    case transaction type of
        1: check type 1
        2: check type 2
        3: check type 3
        4: check type 4
        5: check type 5
        6: check type 6
        else: error 1
    endcase
    dispatch transaction
    read transaction
```

We proceed to the next most difficult expansion in which after checking a type 6 transaction it is saved temporarily:

```
check type 6
    check body 6
    save the transaction 6
    read transaction
    if end of file or not a transaction 7
    then
        error 18
        print transaction 6
        print errors
    else
        six followed by a seven
    endif
```

and the next:

> *six followed by a seven*
> **if** error in transaction 6
> **then**
>> print transaction 6
>> print errors
>> *check type* 7
>> error 19
>
> **else**
>> *check type* 7
>> **if** error in transaction 7
>> **then**
>>> print transaction 6
>>
>> **else**
>>> write transaction 6 to file
>>
>> **endif**
>
> **endif**

By now we are wondering what we have let ourselves in for, and decide we had better sort out:

> *dispatch transaction*
> **if** error
> **then**
>> print transaction
>> print errors
>
> **else**
>> write transaction to file
>
> **endif**

With the distinct feeling that things are much too complicated, we go back to complete the initialization and termination:

> *initialize*
>> open files
>> set error count to zero
>> print heading on report
>> read a transaction
>> set error flag to zero
>
> *complete processing*
>> print footing on report
>> close files

Finally, we deal with the lowest levels of the design:

> *check type* 1
>> check reference number
>> check meter reading
>
> *check type* 2
>> check reference number
>> check payment amount

and so on.

Our assessment of this design is that, while it may very well work, the logic is tortuous. A solution should be sought that is simpler, and that is therefore more likely to work properly and be easier to debug and change.

Up until this point in the development of the program comparatively little time has been spent. However, it may take a considerable time to debug and test a program based on this design. So it is probably well worthwhile to abandon this design and start again from the beginning, in the hope of arriving at a superior design.

5.5 SECOND DESIGN

This solution attempts to deal with the different transaction types in a uniform way. The problem of checking that types 6 and 7 occur in pairs is handled using a flag which always records whether or not the previous transaction was of type 6. Whenever a transaction of type 6 is encountered, it is retained temporarily in order to check the following transaction. We commence as before:

> *validate*
>> *initialize*
>> **perform** *check transaction*
>> **until** end of file
>> *complete processing*
>> stop

Now the **case** construction is completely uniform:

> *check transaction*
>> **case** transaction type **of**
>>> 1: *check type* 1
>>> 2: *check type* 2

> 3: *check type* 3
> 4: *check type* 4
> 5: *check type* 5
> 6: *check type* 6
> 7: *check type* 7
> **else**: error 1
> **endcase**
> **if** transaction type **not** 6
> **then**
>   *dispatch transaction*
> **endif**
> read transaction

What we have done is to back-up to the second level of decomposition and try an alternative expansion, leaving the top level design intact.

On the face of it, the next level of decomposition is straightforward. We must remember that whatever the transaction being examined we must always check the previous one to see whether it is erroneously of type 6.

check type 1
    check previous transaction
    check reference number
    check meter reading

check types 2 *to* 5
    similar to 1

check type 6
    check previous transaction
    check reference number
    check address
    save transaction
    set transaction = 6

check type 7
    if previous transaction was 6
    then
        six then seven
    else
        not six then seven
    endif
    set transaction **not** = 6

But the next stage is horrific! It is even more complex than the first design, being longer and involving more comparisons. It can only be made palatable by keeping a clear head and breaking the solution down into several meaningful, separate program components.

six then seven
    compare reference numbers
    if errors in previous transaction
    then
        error six then seven
    else
        correct six then seven
    endif

not six then seven
    error 18
    check body 7

error six then seven
    print previous transaction
    print errors
    error 19
    check body 7

correct six then seven
    check body 7
    if errors in 7
    then
        print previous transaction
    else
        write previous transaction to file
    endif

check previous transaction
    if previous transaction was 6
    then
        error 18
        print previous transaction
        print errors
    endif
    set transaction **not** = 6

5.6 THIRD DESIGN

Solution 2 above made transactions of type 6 a special case, always saving them until the next card had been examined. The next solution attempts to achieve some simplification by retaining every transaction in a uniform way, so that the current and previous transactions are always available for inspection.

The two messages originally established to describe errors in the sequence of type 6 and 7 transactions were:

18 6 not followed by 7
19 7 preceded by invalid 6

However, in developing this third design it proves necessary during the course of the design to introduce two additional error messages:

20 6 followed by invalid 7
21 7 not preceded by 6

Together these four messages spell out much more clearly the situations that can arise. We get the feeling that this more comprehensive classification of the error situations that has emerged during the design indicates strongly that we are deriving an improved algorithm.

This strategy does indeed result in a simplification of the logic. However, the logic is still complex and in fact needs the use of the following logic decision table to ensure it is correct.

| Previous transaction | *Current transaction* | | |
	Not 7	*Correct 7*	*Error 7*
not 6	normal case	error 21	error 21
correct 6	error 18 in previous	normal case	error 20 in previous
error 6	error 18 in previous	error 19	error 19

This illustrates that using structured programming does not mean that all other techniques are abandoned.

The following design results from this approach. This time it is simplest to back-up to the top level of the design.

validate
    initialize
    perform *check* **until** end of file
    complete processing

check
    switch on transaction type
    dispatch previous transaction
    save transaction
    read transaction

dispatch previous transaction
    if previous transaction exists
    then
        if error in previous transaction
        then
            print previous transaction
            print errors
        else
            write previous transaction to file
        endif
    endif

switch on transaction type
    case transaction type **of**
        1: *check type* 1
        2: *check type* 2
        3: *check type* 3
        4: *check type* 4
        5: *check type* 5
        6: *check type* 6
        7: *check type* 7
    else: error 1
    endcase

initialize
    open files
    set error count to zero
    print heading on report
    set previous transaction does not exist
    read transaction
    set error flag $= 0$

complete processing
   check previous transaction
   dispatch previous transaction
   print footing on report
   close files

check previous transaction
   if previous transaction was 6
   then
      error 18 in previous transaction
   endif

check type 1
   check previous transaction
   check reference number
   check meter reading

check type 6
   check previous transaction
   check reference number
   check address

check type 7
   if previous transaction was 6
   then
      compare reference numbers
      if errors in previous transaction
      then
         error 19
      endif
      check body 7
      if error in 7
      then
         error 20 in previous
      endif
   else
      error 21
      check body
   endif

5.7 FOURTH DESIGN

Solution 3 is fairly simple but has two weaknesses:

(a) Whenever any transaction is processed a check has to be made to see if the previous transaction was a 6. For example, when a type 2 transaction is checked a test is made to see whether the previous transaction was (erroneously) a type 6. There seems to be something intuitively wrong in this; processing type 6 transactions should only be done once, at a single logical place in the program.

(b) The logic that deals with type 7 transactions is complex.

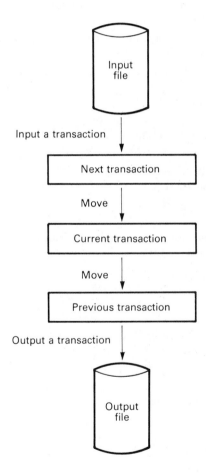

Fig. 5.2 The flow of transactions within the validate program.

The mess can be seen to stem from the fact that when a transaction is being checked, only the immediately previous transaction is available for examination. If, however, not only the previous, but also the next transaction were available it would be possible:

(a)   when processing a 6 to examine the next transaction to see if it is a 7
(b)   when processing a 7, to examine the previous transaction to see if it is a 6.

Therefore, the algorithm given below always maintains three transactions in main store (the data division) for examination—the current, the previous and the next. Fig. 5.2 illustrates this arrangement.

When processing begins there is no "previous" transaction. Similarly when all the file has been checked there is no "next" transaction. So flags are used to describe whether or not each of the three transactions (current, previous, next) exist.

Another change made is to separate completely the checking of individual transactions from the checking of any interdependencies between them, e.g. between 6 and 7.

A very good structure results. The algorithm is short. There are only a few components. Each component carries out a simple well-defined action. Each component is straightforward and involves only a few steps. The design is also one easily capable of extension or modification. For example, it would be easy to alter the design to deal with a new transaction type. Alternatively, if new relationships between transactions were introduced, the changes would be fairly obvious.

The complete solution is presented below, not in the order in which it would have been developed, but in an order which is perhaps more easy to comprehend.

```
validate
    initialize
    perform check until end of file
    complete processing

check
    check next transaction
    check interdependencies of current transaction
    dispatch previous transaction
    move current to previous
    move next to current
    read next
```

check next transaction
  case transaction type **of**
  1: *check type* 1
  2: *check type* 2
  3: *check type* 3
  4: *check type* 4
  5: *check type* 5
  6: *check type* 6
  7: *check type* 7
  else error 1
  endcase

dispatch previous transaction
  if previous transaction exists
  then
    if errors in previous transaction
    then
      print transaction
      print errors
    else
      write transaction to file
    endif
  endif

initialize
  open files
  initialize flags
  print heading on report
  read next transaction
  current transaction does not exist
  previous transaction does not exist

complete processing
  next transaction does not exist
  check interdependencies of current transaction
  dispatch previous transaction
  move current to previous
  dispatch previous transaction
  print footing
  close files

check type 1
  check reference number
  check meter reading

check type 6
   check reference number
   check address

check type 7
   check reference number
   check meter number
   check reading date
   check previous index
   etc.

check interdependencies of current transaction
   if current transaction exists
   then
   case transaction type **of**
      6:   *check interdependencies of* 6
      7:   *check interdependencies of* 7
     else do nothing
   endcase
   endif

check interdependencies of 6
   if next transaction is 7
   then
     if error in next transaction
     then error 20
     endif
   else
     error 18
   endif

check interdependencies of 7
   if previous transaction was 6
   then
     compare reference numbers
     if error in previous transaction
     then error 19
     endif
   else
     error 21
   endif

compare reference numbers
   if reference numbers of
      current and previous transactions
      are not equal
   then
      error 9 in previous transaction
      error 9 in current transaction
   endif

5.8 CONCLUSION

Perhaps you have not followed the twists and turns and discussion of the alternative approaches to designing this program. Or perhaps the optimal design was clear to you from the start. In any case, you must agree that there are alternative solutions to the problem. Each is correct, meaning that it works, but some are better than others, particularly in the sense that they are clearer and easier to maintain.

The use of the structured approach does not divest us of our skill: what it does is to guide us in clearly expressing algorithms and systematically developing them. We still have to devise alternative solutions and decide which amongst them is best. It is tempting to rush on to the coding and testing of a program, but it is vital not to be afraid to discard a weak design and start over from the beginning—it may well save time overall. At the end of the process we have a carefully thought-out product, which we can be confident satisfies the requirements—clarity, simplicity, reliability and ease of modification.

There is a second conclusion to be drawn from the study of this program. It concerns processing a sequential file. We saw earlier in the book that the outline of the structure of a program to process a sequential file is:

process file
   read first record
   perform *process record* **until** end of file
   stop

process record
   deal with record
   read next record

At any one time there is one record in main store (in the DATA DIVISION) and after processing a record the last thing to do in the loop is to read the next record. This is termed reading one record ahead.

In the validate program the simplest design deals with the input of records as follows:

process file
    read first transaction
    current transaction does not exist
    previous transaction does not exist
    perform *check* **until** end of file
    next transaction does not exist
    stop

check
    check transaction
    read next transaction

We see that in this case there are three records held in main store at any one time. This could be expressed by saying that the program reads three records ahead. The program structure reflects the need to check the relationships between every set of three adjoining transactions.

5.9 EXERCISES

1. Most of the complexity in this program arises from the presence of occasional pairs of related records in the file to be processed. Arguably this is a situation where a trivial quirk of the input medium can dictate the entire structure of the program. A way of preventing the structural defect of the input file from affecting the program structure is to hide the actual input structure in an input component. The function of this component is to pass the next logical transaction (valid, invalid or end of file) to the processing component for detailed checking. For this purpose records of types 6 and 7 would be treated as a single logical transaction. Similarly an output component could be constructed to convert logical transactions back into the required records.

    Design a program that utilizes this idea. Is it better than the final design given above?

2. Alter the design given in section 5.7 so that it can cope with batches of transactions, each with a header and a trailer record. Batch header records have a transaction code of 8 and have batch numbers that start at one and increase by one from one batch to the next. A batch trailer record has a transaction code of 9 and contains a field whose value is the number of transactions (not records) in the batch that it terminates.

6

The Design of a Sequential File Update Program

6.1 INTRODUCTION

In Chapter 4 a number of concepts were introduced which could be used to evaluate a program design. Amongst others these included correctness, component size, complexity, coupling and cohesion. The first objective of this chapter is to illustrate how these concepts may be used in the context of the design of a typical data processing problem: the sequential update of a master file with additions, deletions and modifications from a transaction file. A second objective is to develop a generalized algorithm which may be used as a template for the solution of all file update problems regardless of their application area. Although a sequential file update is a very common data processing problem very few published solutions exist which solve the problem in a truly general manner. Most introductory COBOL texts present solutions to a much simplified form of the update which are often difficult to extend to the more general case. For example, many textbook solutions involve a transaction file which is sorted by transaction type within transaction key. Such an ordering often precludes the application of modifications to a newly inserted master record or the reassignment of a record to a master key whose previously assigned record has just been deleted. A general solution should allow any number of transactions of any type and in any sequence to be applied to any particular key value.

The application program developed in this chapter is necessarily a simplified version of a real update. Additional information would normally be contained in the master file and many additional transactions would be required. All the ingredients for discussion of sequential updates in general are, however, present.

6.2   THE PROGRAM SPECIFICATION

A small telephone company requires a billing system for its customer accounts. The company keeps a master file of customer records detailing for each customer such information as phone number, name, billing address, basic monthly charge, and account balance. The file is sequentially organized and ordered on the key field phone number.

The company has installed a system which automatically monitors all telephone calls, generating information such as the origin of the call, the destination, the date and duration of the call and its computed cost. The details of each call are posted to an account transactions file where they accumulate until they are applied, once a month, to the master file. The update modifies the customer accounts and generates a billing file which is later used to send monthly statements of account to customers. Other transactions, generated by events such as the receipt of a customer payment or the closing of a customer account, are also posted to the same accounts transaction file as they are received by the company. The company's transaction entry system assigns a unique serial number to each transaction as it is posted to the transaction file. This serial number reflects the time order in which the transactions were posted in the file.

Program description:
A monthly update program is required which applies the transactions to the master file producing:

(a)   a *billing file* which contains information necessary for the generation of customers' monthly statements. Statements are mailed to customers on preprinted stationery by a subsequent billing program;

(b)   a new *updated master file* reflecting the transactions applied to the original master file;

(c)   a *closed account file* which contains summaries of accounts which were closed during the update;

(d)   an *update log report* which details all transactions which, for any reason, were rejected and not applied to the master file during the update.

Computer run diagram:

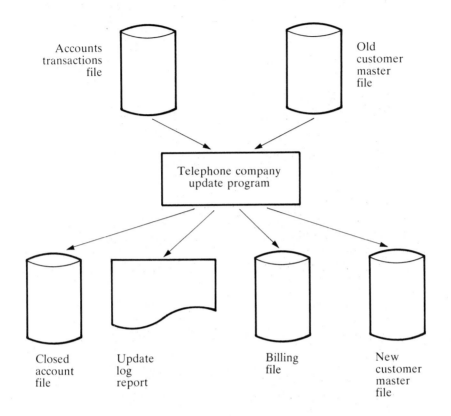

Input file(s):

Old customer master file

Sequentially organized
Sorted by ascending telephone number
Records in the file are formatted as shown below:

Phone number	
region code	999
area code	999
local number	9999
Customer name	X(30)
Billing address	X(60)
Basic monthly charge	9(4)V99
Account balance	S9(6)V99

Accounts transactions file (4 Record types)

Sequentially organized
Sorted by ascending transaction serial number within ascending telephone number.
Records are formatted according to their transaction type as shown below:

(a)   Insertion
        phone number   9(10)
        transaction serial number   9(9)
        transaction type   X   *(Value="I")*
        customer name   X(30)
        billing address   X(60)
        basic monthly charge   9(4)V99

(b)   Deletion
        phone number   9(10)
        transaction serial number   9(9)
        transaction type   X   *(Value = "D")*
        deletion date   DDMMYY   *(e.g. 210781)*

(c)   Customer payment
        phone number   9(10)
        transaction serial number   9(9)
        transaction type   X   *(Value = "P")*
        amount received   S9(6)V99
        date   DDMMYY

(d)   Phone calls
        originating phone number   9(10)
        transaction serial number   9(9)
        transaction type   X   *(Value = "C")*
        destination phone number   9(10)
        date of call   DDMMYY
        duration of call (e.g. 0105 for HHMM
        1 *hour* 5 *mins*)
        cost of call   9(4)V99

Output file(s):

Billing file

Sequentially organized
Ordered on ascending telephone number
May contain records with the same telephone number if more than one customer has an outstanding account on that telephone number.

Phone number	9(10)
Customer name	X(30)
Billing address	X(60)
Basic monthly charge	9(4)V99
Opening balance	S9(6)V99
Cost of calls made	9(6)V99
Payments this month	S9(6)V99
Tax this month	9(6)V99
Closing account balance	S9(6)V99

Closed account file

Sequentially organized
Ordered by telephone number
May contain records with duplicate telephone numbers
Each record contains an account summary for any accounts which were closed during updating operations.

Phone number	9(10)
Customer name	X(30)
Customer address	X(60)
Closing date	999999
Closing balance	S9(6)V99

Update log report

Suitably formatted details of rejected transactions and the reason for their rejection.

New customer master file

See details of old customer master file.

Program details:

Transactions are to be applied to the master file in the order in which they appear within the account transactions file.

Each transaction in the accounts transaction file has been previously validated, as far as is possible without requiring examination of the customer master file. The update program should carry out all remaining checks for invalid transactions.

Multiple transactions may be applied to the same master record. All logically sound transaction sequences are to be allowed. For example, in the same update run, it should be possible for an existing customer to have a payment processed, an account closed, and subsequently for a new customer to be allocated to the original phone number. On the other hand, it would be an error to apply a deletion transaction for a phone number that is not currently allocated to any customer.

For each valid insertion transaction a new master record is generated using the information contained within the transaction. In addition, the account balance will be set to zero.

For each valid deletion transaction a summary of account is generated and output to the closed account file. Also, a closing statement of account is output to the billing file provided the account has a non-zero closing balance. A master file record with this phone number will not appear in the new master file unless the number is subsequently reallocated to another customer and remains so allocated at the end of the update.

For each valid payment transaction the amount received is added to a cumulative total which computes the total payments made against the account this month.

For each valid phone call transaction the cost of the call is added to a cumulative total which computes the total cost of all calls charged to the account this month.

For all master file accounts which are "active" after the application of all transactions (if any) to the account a record detailing the overall monthly account activity (cost of calls made, total payments received) is output to the billing file. The closing account balance (including any tax payable) is computed and included in the billing record. This balance is included in the new master file record for the account. Billing records are not generated for accounts with zero closing balances.

All rejected transactions are detailed in the update log report.

All payments received to clear outstanding balances on closed accounts are handled separately and are *not* included within the account transactions file.

6.3   SEQUENTIAL UPDATE FUNDAMENTALS

The updating of information within a sequential file to reflect changes that have taken place is a very common data processing application. Regardless of any particular application area, all sequential file updates exhibit the following common characteristics:

A master file contains a collection of information relevant to a particular application, for example, account information records for the customers of the telephone company. The records in the master file are ordered on a key field whose value uniquely identifies an individual record, for example, the customer phone number.

Periodically, the status of the information in the master file must be updated. This is usually done by collecting or batching together the updates required into a transactions file which is then sorted on the same key field as the master file. The update may be carried out on a daily, weekly, or monthly basis depending on the level of transaction activity and how often the master file is to be used as a basis for management decision making.

By a sequential update we mean that every single record in the master file will be accessed in the course of each update run and that the update will result in the creation of a completely new master file. This mode of operation is most efficient where the majority of master file records are modified during each update. When speed is of paramount importance, requiring that transactions must be applied to the master file immediately they occur, or when only a small number of master file records will be modified on any update run, the master file would be organized randomly. A random update retrieves only those records actually requiring modification and the update is carried out "in place", that is, by modifying the original master file. This mode of updating requires that the master file be accessed from a direct access storage device.

Although, in any particular application, there may be any number of events which necessitate an update to the master file, each transaction will fall into one of only three types, insertions (add a new record to the file), deletions (remove a record from the file) and changes (modify a record in some way).

Records in the transaction file will almost certainly have been validated for data inconsistencies. However, the update should recognize and reject transactions which prove to be invalid when the master file is consulted. For example, a change or deletion transaction applied to a non-existent record or an attempt to insert a record with the same key as an existing record.

In any particular file update run, nil, one, or many transactions can be applied to an individual master file record.

6.4 AN INITIAL ALGORITHM

Before developing a solution to the telephone company update we will examine the general logic required to implement a simple sequential update involving insertions, deletions and changes.

Since both the master and transactions files are ordered on the same key field, a possible approach would be to base the update logic on an algorithm for merging together two input files into a single output file where matches, or records with the same key values, may exist within the input files. That is, both the master and transaction files will be accessed sequentially, using a "read-ahead" technique, and the keys of the current transaction and master records compared. There are now three possibilities. If the keys are equal then we should have a change or deletion transaction. If the transaction key is less than the master key then an insertion transaction should be present, and finally, if the transaction key is greater than the master key then the master record may be copied to the new master file as no more transactions will be posted against that record. Whenever a transaction or master record has been completely processed the next record is read from that file to maintain the "read-ahead". Records are read from each file until one or other of the files becomes empty. If we further arrange that whenever the end of the file is reached on either input file, the key returned by the read routine for that file is a sentinel value greater than any valid key, the basic key comparison logic can be continued until both files are empty. Refining this algorithm to include logic to identify and reject invalid transactions we arrive at the following algorithm:

> *update sequential master file*
>> *initialize*
>> *read a transaction record*
>> *read an old master record*
>> **perform** *update operations*
>>> **until** both transaction and master files are empty
>> *terminate*

> *update operations*
>> **if** old master key < transaction key
>> **then**
>>> *copy old master record to new master file*
>>> *read an old master record*
>> **else if** old master key = transaction key
>>> **then**
>>>> **case** transaction type **of**
>>>>> insertion   :   *duplicate insertion error*
>>>>> change   :   *apply change to old master record*
>>>>> deletion   :   *read an old master record*
>>>> **endcase**

> *read a transaction*
> **else if** old master key > transaction key
> > **then**
> > > **case** transaction type **of**
> > > > insertion : *copy record to be inserted to master file*
> > > > change   : *unmatched transaction error*
> > > > deletion   : *unmatched transaction error*
> > > **endcase**
> > > *read a transaction*
> > **endif**
> **endif**
endif

read a transaction
> read the next transaction record
> **if** end of file was encountered
> **then**
> > set transaction key to sentinel value
> **endif**

read an old master record
> read the next old master record
> **if** end of file was encountered
> **then**
> > set old master key to sentinel value
> **endif**

Have we developed the skeleton of an algorithm which could be used as a template for all sequential updates? For example, would this algorithm be appropriate as a template for the telephone company example?

6.5 THE INITIAL ALGORITHM REVIEWED

The importance of checking the correctness and quality of a program design at each stage of its development cannot be overstressed. It is well worth remembering that the earlier design flaws or inefficiencies are discovered the less expensive they are to rectify. Before considering the suitability of the algorithm, we should criticize the way in which its design evolved. One of our guidelines was that the design process should be carried out in a series of small steps. In our example, far too many design decisions have been made in a single decomposition. For example, basic design decisions have been taken with regard to:

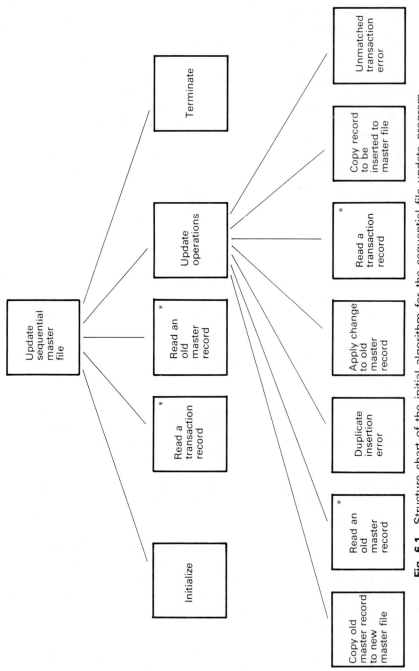

Fig. 6.1 Structure chart of the initial algorithm for the sequential file update program.

(a) the technique to be used to read individual records from both input files;
(b) the use of a sentinel value to facilitate end of file processing;
(c) the comparison of master and transaction key fields to determine transaction processing;
(d) the recognition of invalid transactions.

If we study the structure chart corresponding to the design (Fig. 6.1) we see that "update operations" has seven subordinate modules. As we mentioned earlier this is often, although not always, a sign of a poor decomposition. It suggests that the module has to exercise control over too many modules and is thus too complex. Such modules often also exhibit low functional cohesion. A good test for a functionally cohesive module is to look at its decomposition and judge whether or not it is simple to conclude that the components carry out the single recognizable task associated with the name of the module. In the case of the "update operations" module, there are too many components, and they are too detailed and too diverse in nature to recognize immediately the task they collectively perform.

Of course, these faults could be remedied simply by splitting the module into a smaller number of higher level components which can themselves be refined. The effect of this on the structure chart is to lower the output span of "update operations" and increase the number of levels in the decomposition of the module. Far more serious, however, is the discovery that the algorithm itself is incorrect. Though in some simpler, restricted, update applications the initial algorithm presented may be adequate, it contains a number of serious flaws which preclude its use as a general standard.

For example, one of the characteristics of updates we quoted earlier was that for any individual master file key, zero, one or many transactions may be applied during a single update run. No mention was made, nor should it have been, of any restrictions in the sequence of transactions allowed for any particular key value. Although the initial algorithm handles some common multiple transaction sequences correctly (e.g. a sequence of changes to an existing record), problems arise for certain other sequences. For example, since insertion transactions are applied immediately, resulting in a new record being placed in the new master file, we are restricted from applying change or delete transactions to an inserted record. For similar reasons, multiple insertions on the same key value would be undetected by the algorithm and result in records with duplicate keys appearing in the new master file.

A general update algorithm should accept any number of transactions of any type and in any sequence for any particular key value. Of course, some transactions should be recognized as illegal. For example, attempting to delete a record at a time when no record is currently associated with that key.

Logically sound but quite complex transaction sequences are, however, possible. An acceptable sequence of events for a customer account of the telephone company might consist of any number of payments and phone call transactions, followed by a request to close the account and the subsequent reallocation of the account (i.e. same phone number) to a new customer.

Another consideration raised by the last example is the importance of ensuring that transactions are presented in the actual order in which they occur. For instance, in the previous example, had a phone call made by the previous customer not been posted until after the closure of the account then the new customer would be billed for that call. To preserve the validity of the update, a transactions file should be sorted on the master file key field and where multiple transactions occur on the same key they must be presented in the order in which the events took place.

When a review of a design casts a shadow over its quality or, more seriously, reveals actual design flaws, the designer must modify the existing design or possibly make a completely fresh start. Retracing the steps taken to arrive at the current design will reveal the level of the design below which modification or redesign is necessary but above which the original design remains sound and can be retained intact. In our case, redesign is necessary from the top level.

We have stated many times already that program design is a difficult process. We cannot always expect to arrive at a nearly optimal solution at the first design attempt. Often a design review will leave us with the feeling that, although our initial design seems adequate, we could do better given a second opportunity. Although circumstances, such as deadlines, may preclude redesign, the additional time and effort taken to improve the design will be repaid many times over the total lifetime of the program.

6.6   AN IMPROVED ALGORITHM

The initial algorithm did not give due consideration to the fact that, during the course of an update, the status of a particular key may change several times and that the logical correctness of any transaction can be determined only by examining the status of the key at the time the transaction is to be applied. The status of a key is said to be allocated if an active master file record is currently associated with that key and unallocated otherwise.

An improved algorithm, described in Dwyer,[1] can be obtained if the program logic is driven by the processing of transactions from the transaction file. The sorted transaction file can be thought of as consisting of a set of sequences of transactions of length one or more, where each sequence groups together transactions relating to a particular key. Consequently the algorithm should process each key for which there exists a transaction sequence. For each sequence the initial status for that key can be determined, then each transaction applied, possibly altering the key's status. If the final status of the key is allocated, the record will be copied to the new master file.

We must also deal with those keys in the old master file for which there are no transactions and which should be copied to the new master file unchanged. The algorithm is modified to process all keys which appear either in the transaction or old master file, selecting the smaller of the two current keys at each stage. No further modification of the algorithm is required. The transaction processing nature of the algorithm is retained by considering those master file keys for which there are no transactions as having a sequence of zero transactions applied against them. As the status of these keys will continue to be allocated, the records associated with them will be copied to the new master file.

Retaining the use of a sentinel key value from the initial algorithm whenever end of file is encountered on either input file we arrive at the following algorithm:

> *update sequential master file*
>> open files
>> *read a transaction record*
>> *read an old master record*
>> *choose the next key to process*
>> **perform** *process transaction sequence on next key*
>>> **until** current key = sentinel
>> close files
>
> *process transaction sequence on next key*
>> *obtain initial status of current key*
>> **perform** *process a transaction on the current key*
>>> **until** transaction key **not** = current key
>> *check final status of current key*
>> *choose the next key to process*
>
> *read a transaction record*
>> read the next transaction record
>> **if** end of file was encountered
>> **then**
>>> set transaction key = sentinel
>> **endif**
>
> *read an old master record*
>> read the next old master record
>> **if** end of file was encountered

> **then**
>> set old master key = sentinel
> **endif**

> *choose the next key to process*
> **if** transaction key < old master key
> **then**
>> set current key = transaction key
> **else**
>> set current key = old master key
> **endif**

The component *obtain initial status of current key* determines whether or not the current key is allocated, and if so, copies the old master into a work area referred to as the current master and immediately reads the next old master to conform with our "read ahead" technique. Subsequent transactions, of whatever type, will now have the effect of modifying either or both the current master record and the status of the current key.

> *obtain initial status of current key*
> **if** old master key = current master key
> **then**
>> set current master to old master
>> set status of current key to allocated
>> *read an old master record*
> **else**
>> set status of current key to unallocated
> **endif**

Process a transaction on the current key applies a transaction to the current master and then reads the next transaction.

> *process a transaction on the current key*
>> *apply transaction to current master*
>> *read a transaction record*

The component *check final status of current key* determines whether the current key is allocated after the application of all transactions, if any, to the key. If the key is allocated the current master is copied to the new master file.

> *check final status of current key*
> **if** status of current key is allocated
> **then**
>> *copy current master record to new master file*
> **endif**

The component *apply transaction to current master* applies individual transactions to the current master. The logical correctness of each transaction is checked by examining the status of the current key when the transaction is to be applied. For example, if we have an insertion transaction and the current key is allocated we have an error.

> *apply transaction to current master*
>   **case** transaction type **of**
>   insertion   : *process insertion transaction*
>   deletion   : *process deletion transaction*
>   change   : *process change transaction*
>   **endcase**
>
> *process insertion transaction*
>   **if** status of current key is allocated
>   **then**
>   *duplicate insertion error*
>   **else**
>   *create current master from insertion transaction information*
>   set status of current key to allocated
>   **endif**
>
> *process deletion transaction*
>   **if** status of current key is **not** allocated
>   **then**
>   *unmatched transaction error*
>   **else**
>   set status of current key to unallocated
>   **endif**
>
> *process change transaction*
>   **if** status of current key is **not** allocated
>   **then**
>   *unmatched transaction error*
>   **else**
>   *apply changes required to current master*
>   **endif**

6.7 THE IMPROVED ALGORITHM REVIEWED

To design an algorithm which can be used as a template for many sequential file update applications, we must be particularly vigilant to ensure that we have a quality design. This gives us an opportunity to discuss further

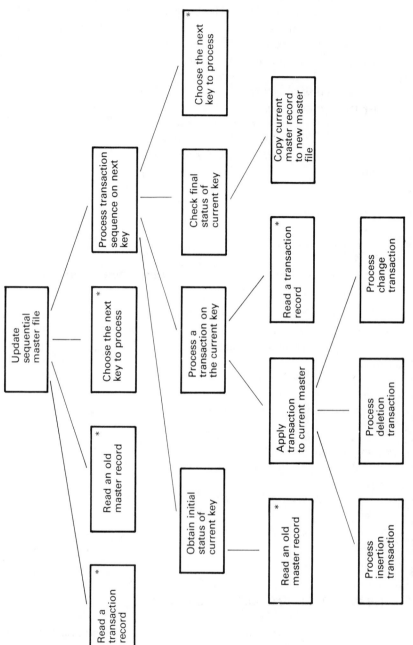

Fig. 6.2   Structure chart of the improved algorithm for the sequential file update program.

the criteria which can be applied to a program design to obtain some measure of its quality. These include component size and complexity, the topology of the structure chart, and cohesion and coupling.

Component Size and Complexity

Each component of the algorithm consists of a small number of statements, and, just as importantly, the logic structures within each component are simple.

The Topology of the Structure Chart

The structure chart for the improved algorithm is shown in Fig. 6.2. What features of the structure chart are important? We stated earlier that short, fat structures, where components have a large number of subordinates, are often an indication that a component is too complex; having to exercise control over too many others. The inverse, tall, thin structures whose components have only one or two subordinates are often quite normal decomposition structures, though in excess, they too can be signals of a poor design structure. In most instances, as in the case of the chart shown in Fig. 6.2, we should not expect to see modules with excessively large numbers of subordinates.

Cohesion and Coupling

The measurement of cohesion and coupling within a design can be a significant indicator of the ease with which a design will stand up to modification. Ideally, we would like to have highly cohesive and loosely coupled components. This will ensure that there is a high degree of interaction between the statements within each component and a minimum of interaction between components.

All components should be functionally cohesive, the most desirable of Constantine's levels of cohesion. Such components will contain statements which are strongly interrelated and which can collectively be clearly seen to achieve the single task associated with the name of the component. Our goal should be to ensure that all components of a design are strongly cohesive. What is important, therefore, is to look at each component, gain some measure of its strength, and, if it is not highly cohesive, either justify its present design or redesign it in a more cohesive manner. Poorly cohesive components are often quite easy to identify. Common examples are components which contain statements which are obviously unrelated to one another (coincidental cohesion), or which perform independent, but logically similar functions (logical cohesion).

Before considering the cohesion of our present design we should note that, so far, our structure charts have been constructed so that a strict one-to-one correspondence between components in our pseudocode and components of the structure chart is maintained. This seems a very desirable goal but can have some unfortunate consequences. Earlier we decided not to use in-line repetition structures in our pseudocode. This allowed us to use a pseudocode notation that would allow easy translation into COBOL. It also means, however, that the pseudocode, and hence our structure charts, contain components which are not truly necessary. For example, the component *process transaction on the current key* would not have appeared in the design if *process a transaction sequence on the current key* had been initially decomposed as shown below:

> *process a transaction sequence on the current key*
>   *obtain initial status of current key*
> **perform**
>   *apply transaction to current master*
>   *read a transaction record*
> **until** transaction key **not** = current key
>   *check final status of current key*
>   *choose the next key to process*

Inclusion of components which really represent only loop bodies can make structure charts for large programs unnecessarily complicated. Consequently, some programmers do not include them in the structure chart. Indeed, when designing large programs, an overall structure chart can be used to develop a basic design strategy before any pseudocode is developed. If we do include these artificial components, we should be somewhat lenient when evaluating their cohesion. These components are often procedurally cohesive. The statements within such components correspond to the sequence of operations appearing within a section of the program. As procedurally cohesive components exhibit less than optimum cohesion, we should not implement them in COBOL as separately compiled subprograms.

Some components within our design, for example, *choose the next key to process*, *read a transaction record*, and *read an old master record* display high levels of cohesion. However, the components *obtain initial status of current key* and *check final status of current key* can be improved by choosing a name more representative of the functions they perform. Currently it appears that functions such as maintaining "read ahead" on the old master file and copying the current master to the new master file are side-effects of these components. We choose to name them *initiate processing of current key* and *terminate processing of current key* respectively.

Coupling is strongly related to cohesion; a design with highly cohesive components will almost always have loosely coupled components. Coupling is a measure of the strength of the interactions between components in a design. Loosely coupled components ensure that components will be highly independent, thus minimizing the likelihood that a change in one component

will have an impact on another. The coupling between any pair of components can be measured by finding the set of data items common to both. For
example, the component *choose the next key to process* has the following
interface with components which invoke it. Given the data items transaction
key and old master key, the component returns the data item current key to
the calling component. This component is therefore loosely coupled to all
other components in the design. In a similar fashion we can measure the
coupling between all pairs of components in the design. The coupling between components can be conveniently displayed by extending the structure
chart to contain interface details. For example, the interface between *process transaction sequence on next key* and *choose the next key to process* could
be shown thus:

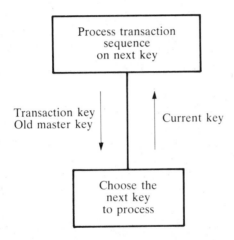

We leave it as an exercise for the reader to complete the annotation of
the structure chart with coupling information. Note that we have implicitly
assumed that there will be no coupling between components that do not
invoke each other. This is not necessarily the case. A pair of components not
connected to each other in the structure chart can be coupled because they
both refer to some shared data.

Most modern programming languages offer data control facilities which
allow components to be treated as "black boxes" with controlled communication to the outside world only possible through a well specified interface.
We will discuss this topic further with respect to COBOL in Chapter 8.

6.8 A SOLUTION TO THE TELEPHONE COMPANY PROBLEM

In this section we examine how the generalized sequential update
algorithm may be customized to meet the requirements of the telephone
company problem. As is typical of most business application update programs, a good deal of ancillary processing is required in addition to the basic

updating operations. In our example, a billing file, containing information for subsequent use by a customer billing program, and a closed account file, containing summary information relating to accounts closed during the update, are required in addition to an updated master file and update log. The update algorithm template provides an invaluable framework around which solutions to complex real-life application updates can be constructed.

The high level logic of the update algorithm requires little modification. The telephone company update involves four transaction types, to insert a new account, to close or delete an account, to record a customer payment and to record a phone call. The processing required for each transaction type need not concern us at this stage.

The component *read a transaction record* reads the next transaction, extracting the field phone number as the transaction key. If end of file is encountered the transaction key is set to a sentinel value. *Read an old master record* operates in an entirely similar way to read the next record from the old master file and set the old master key. The components *update sequential master file* and *choose the next key to process* require no modification.

```
update sequential master file
    open files
    read a transaction record
    read an old master record
    choose the next key to process
    perform process transaction sequence on next key
        until current key = sentinel
    close files

read a transaction record
    read the next transaction record
    if end of file was encountered
    then
        set transaction key = sentinel
    else
        set transaction key = transaction phone number
    endif

read an old master record
    read the next old master record
    if end of file was encountered
    then
        set old master key = sentinel
    else
        set old master key = old master phone number
    endif
```

choose the next key to process
    if transaction key < old master key
    then
        set current key = transaction key
    else
        set current key = old master key
    endif

In order that monthly statements of account may be sent to customers, the program specification requires that a monthly activity record be generated for each customer account written to the new master file. The activity record will accumulate all payments received and chargeable phone calls made during the month. This will permit calculation of any tax payable and determination of the final balance.

The simplest method of accomplishing this function is to modify the algorithm to create a null or initially empty activity record whenever a key becomes allocated. Subsequent payment and phone call transactions, if any, will amend this activity record.

Provided the key remains allocated after all transactions have been applied, the account balance may be updated and the customer account written to the new master file. If, in addition, the account balance is non-zero then the monthly activity record is written to the billing file.

The template algorithm is modified to reflect the additional application processing required prior to and following the processing of a transaction sequence for a key.

process transaction sequence on next key
    initiate processing of current key
    perform *process a transaction on the current key*
        until transaction key **not** = current key
    terminate processing of current key
    choose the next key to process

initiate processing of current key
    if old master key = current master key
    then
        set current master to old master
        set status of current key to allocated
        create monthly activity record for current key
        read an old master record
    else
        set status of current key to unallocated
    endif

> *process a transaction on the current key*
>   *apply transaction to current master*
>   *read a transaction record*
>
> *terminate processing of current key*
>   **if** status of current key is allocated
>   **then**
>   *calculate closing account balance*
>   *update current master balance*
>   **if** current master balance **not** zero
>   **then**
>   *send monthly activity record to billing file*
>   **endif**
>   *copy current master record to new master file*
>   **endif**

The application dependent transaction processing routines can now be added. The identification of invalid transactions and the resetting of the status of the current key, if necessary, remains unchanged. Valid phone call and payment transactions update the monthly activity record for that key. Valid insertion transactions create a current master record from the transaction details and a new activity record is created to instigate the generation of billing information for the new account. The closing balance is calculated for valid deletion transactions and a summary of the account details is recorded in the closed account file. In addition, the monthly activity record is recorded in the billing file.

> *apply transaction to current master*
>   **case** transaction type **of**
>   insertion   :   *process insertion transaction*
>   deletion   :   *process deletion transaction*
>   phone call   :   *process phone call transaction*
>   payment   :   *process payment transaction*
>   **endcase**
>
> *process insertion transaction*
>   **if** status of current key is allocated
>   **then**
>   *send duplicate insertion error record to update log*
>   **else**
>   *create current master from insertion transaction information*
>   set status of current key to allocated
>   *create monthly activity record for current key*
>   **endif**

process deletion transaction
    if status of current key is **not** allocated
    then
        send unmatched transaction error record to update log
    else
        calculate closing account balance
        update current master balance
        send summary of account to closed account file
        if closed account balance **not** zero
        then
            send monthly activity record to billing file
        endif
        set status of current key to unallocated
    endif

process phone call transaction
    if status of current key is **not** allocated
    then
        send unmatched transaction error record to update log
    else
        update monthly activity record with phone call details
    endif

process payment transaction
    if status of current key is **not** allocated
    then
        send unmatched transaction error record to update log
    else
        update monthly activity record with payment details
    endif

The computation required to calculate any tax payable and the closing balances for an account is left to the reader.

6.9 CUSTOMIZING THE GENERAL ALGORITHM

We have seen how the sequential update algorithm template can be readily customized to fit a particular application. In this section we discuss a number of common situations prevalent in update programs and show how the template may be modified to deal with them.

In some applications, logical dependencies may exist between transactions. A common example occurs when several physical transaction input records are used to describe a single logical transaction. In this situation, the component *read a transaction record* should be modified so that it always returns all the information required to process any logical transaction. For example, suppose in the telephone company problem, the insertion transaction had been split between two successive input transactions as shown below:

Insertion (Record 1)		Insertion (Record 2)	
Phone number	7(10)	Phone number	9(10)
Transaction serial number	9(9)	Transaction serial number	9(9)
Transaction type (value = "I")	X	Transaction type (value = "I")	X
Customer name	X(30)	Billing address	X(60)
Basic monthly charge	9(6)V99		

Assuming that the insertion transaction record pairs have been previously validated the component *read a transaction record* can be customized as follows:

> *read a transaction record*
>> read the next transaction record
>> **if** end of file was encountered
>> **then**
>>> set transaction key = sentinel
>> **else**
>>> set transaction key = transaction phone number
>>> **if** transaction type = insertion
>>> **then**
>>>> read the next transaction record
>>>> merge the input record pair to form a logical insertion transaction
>>> **endif**
>> **endif**

Similar customization techniques can be used to control logical dependencies between records in the master file. The physical structure of the master file will often be optimized by the systems designer to minimize the total amount of storage space taken up by records in the file.

For example, the records in the telephone company problem are sorted on the ten digit key field phone number, where each key is structured to consist of a three digit region code, a three digit area code and finally a four digit local number. We can expect, given a reasonable percentage of allocated keys, that the first six digits of a key will be constant for a sizeable group of consecutive master file records. To avoid storing the common portion of the key on each record, the master file could be reorganized to consist of two types of records; group header and customer detail records.

The master file is now structured as a set of record groups where each group consists of a group header record followed by a variable number of customer detail records all of which have the same initial six digits for their key as those specified in the group header record.

Customization of the algorithm to deal with structured master files can be accomplished with a minimum of disruption if we keep in mind that, regardless of the physical record structure, we wish to process logical records, that is, the collection of information associated with each key. In our example, a logical record is simply the concatenation of a group header and a customer detail record. Customization is achieved by modifying the algorithm components *initiate processing of current key* and *terminate processing of current key*. The fact that only these two components require modification is testimony to the high degree of module independence we achieved in our algorithm. The implementation of this customization is left for the reader.

Inglis[2] describes a problem that arises when the basic update algorithm is used in an environment where transactions are generated by many users of a system. Assume an insertion transaction on a particular key is rejected because the key is currently allocated. Now, if this insertion transaction were followed by several other change or delete transactions on the same key, it will not be clear to which master file record, the existing one or the rejected one, the transactions should be applied. In the worst case, these transactions might be a mixture, some for the original and some for the rejected replacement. We cannot be sure which master file record each individual user of the system intended to use.

What happens when such a transaction sequence is input to our basic update algorithm? The insertion transaction will be correctly rejected but subsequent transactions will be assumed, possibly incorrectly, to refer to the original master file record. Clearly, these transactions should not be applied while such ambiguity is present.

One solution to this problem would be to provide additional information within the transactions themselves to ensure that all ambiguities can be immediately resolved—an expensive and unwieldy solution. A better approach, described by Inglis, is to mark as suspended any master file record to which an invalid insertion transaction is applied, and to subsequently ensure that the only transaction which can be applied to suspended or deactivated records is a transaction to reactivate them. This additional transaction is used when the ambiguity within the original transaction sequence has been resolved and the transactions are ready for resubmission.

The modifications required to the basic algorithm are shown below. Only those components dealing with the processing of individual transactions require modification. An additional transaction type, to reactivate a suspended master file record, is introduced. Note also, that an entry must be provided in each logical master record to store its status (suspended or not) and that it is an error to attempt to reactivate a master record which is not suspended.

> *apply transaction to current master*
> **case** transaction type **of**
>   insertion   :   *process insertion transaction*
>   deletion   :   *process deletion transaction*
>   change   :   *process change transaction*
>   restore record status   :   *process restore status transaction*
> **endcase**

> *process insertion transaction*
>   **if** status of current key is allocated
>   **then**
>   *duplicate insertion error*
>   set current master to be suspended
>   **else**
>   *create current master from insertion transaction information*
>   set status of current key to allocated
>   **endif**

> *process deletion transaction*
>   **if** status of current key is **not** allocated
>   **then**
>   *unmatched transaction error*
>   **else if** current master is **not** suspended
>   **then**
>   set status of key to unallocated
>   **else**
>   *reject transaction—master currently suspended*
>   **endif**
>   **endif**

> *process change transaction*
>   **if** status of current key is **not** allocated
>   **then**
>   *unmatched transaction error*
>   **else if** current master is **not** suspended
>   **then**
>   *apply changes required to current master*
>   **else**
>   *reject transaction—master currently suspended*
>   **endif**
>   **endif**

process restore status transaction
  if status of current key is unallocated
  then
    unmatched transaction error
  else if current master is **not** suspended
    then
      *reject transaction—master **not** currently suspended*
    else
      set current master to be **not** suspended
    endif
  endif

6.10 SUMMARY

The characteristics of a very common data processing problem, a sequential file update, have been studied. A general algorithm has been developed which could be adopted as a standard template by a programming installation and can be refined to meet the needs of a particular application. We have discussed how a number of criteria, including component size and complexity, the topology of the structure chart, and cohesion and coupling, may be used to evaluate a program design. We have shown how the template algorithm can be customized to solve a typical update problem and discussed how the algorithm may be modified to deal with some of the more commonly occurring complexities to be found in commercial file updating operations.

6.11 ACKNOWLEDGMENTS

The updating algorithm discussed in this chapter was first developed by W. H. J. Feijen and described by Dijkstra.[3] An eloquent discussion of update programs by Dwyer[1] describes the derivation of a general updating algorithm, the translation of the algorithm into COBOL and the adaptation of the algorithm to deal with the additional complexities of real-life updates. Inglis[2] discusses solutions to the problem of invalid insertions being subsequently followed by additional transactions on the same key in a multi-user environment.

6.12 REFERENCES

1. Dwyer, B. "One More Time—How to Update a Master File", *Comm. ACM*, **24** (1), (1981), pp.3–8.

2. Inglis, J. "Updating a Master File—Yet One More Time", *Comm. ACM*, **24** (5), (1981), p.299.

3. Dijkstra, E. W. *A Discipline of Programming*, Prentice-Hall, Englewood Cliffs, N.J., 1976, Chapter 15.

6.13 EXERCISES

1. Most COBOL programming textbooks and many texts on program design include examples of sequential file update programs. Examine the update logic contained within some of these textbook examples and try to ascertain whether, firstly, the update logic is correct, and secondly, whether the presented algorithm places unnecessary restrictions on possible updating operations.

2. The following specification change is proposed for the telephone company program.
    A new transaction transfer account is to be instigated to allow customers to transfer their existing accounts to a new phone number when, for instance, they change residence. The transaction has the format:

Existing phone number	9(10)
Transaction serial number	9(9)
Transaction type	X (Value = "T")
New phone number	9(10)

    What problems, if any, do you foresee in implementing the processing of this new transaction?

3. Amend the algorithm for the telephone company problem to include the following specification changes:
    (a) The master file is to be reorganized to consist of two types of records, group header and customer detail records, as described in Section 6.9. No empty record groups are to be allowed within the master file. That is, each group header record must be followed by at least one customer detail record.
    (b) Sequence checking of both the transaction and master files is required.

4. To improve the service to their customers the telephone company has decided to use the information held within the accounts transaction file to provide a detailed billing breakdown of each call made by a customer.
    Redesign the layout of the billing file and amend the update algorithm so that the billing program will be capable of detailing for each call:
    (a) the phone number called
    (b) the date of the call
    (c) the duration of the call
    (d) the cost of the call.

5. Develop an algorithm which could be used as a template for update programs involving master files which allow random rather than sequential access to individual records. Is the algorithm substantially different from that presented for sequentially organized files?

7

Making the most of COBOL

7.1 INTRODUCTION

This chapter gives a description of a subset of COBOL. It is intended for two kinds of people. First, those with a knowledge of programming, but not of COBOL. For such readers we present a brief outline of the language. Second, an experienced COBOL programmer, who might like to read this chapter to see a stripped-down version of COBOL that we suggest as being a suitable basis for good coding. Alternatively, such readers could skip this chapter.

COBOL is a very "big" language—it has many verbs and options. The manual for COBOL on a particular machine is usually forbiddingly long. The American National standard is $1\frac{1}{4}''$ thick. It is virtually impossible to learn the whole language and reference to the manual is often necessary to confirm the action of particular language facilities. We suggest that the use of a language that is not fully understood must lead to errors. True, we can always consult the manual, but this in itself is not only time-consuming but prone to errors. We suggest that a good way round this particular problem is to restrict ourselves to a subset of the language and stick to it. This subset is sufficiently powerful to enable most tasks to be carried out, but small enough to be fully understood by the programmer. Following this strategy means ignoring certain "powerful" facilities that are useful occasionally, but if our goal is clarity in order to promote reliability and ease of maintenance it may well be worth it.

In this chapter we suggest a usable subset of COBOL. We take the view that it is better to describe what we can do rather than to list what we should not do. If you are familiar with the language and we have omitted one of your

113

favorite facilities, please ask yourself the following questions before you get annoyed with us:

(a)   Is it really necessary (or is it a frill that clutters up the language)?

(b)   Does it contribute towards program clarity?

We confine ourselves to the international standard for COBOL, ANSI X3.23 – 1974.

7.2   PROGRAM LAYOUT

The text of a COBOL program is written in columns 8 to 72 inclusive. Columns 8 to 11 inclusive are known as area A, columns 12 to 72 as area B. Certain things must be written so that they start in area A; other elements must not appear in area A. Another niggling rule is that the arithmetic operators +, −, *, /, and ** must be preceded and followed by a space. Otherwise COBOL is completely free format: statements can be indented to start anywhere; spaces and blank lines can appear anywhere. This flexibility can be used to aid the readability of a program.

One very useful facility is that by writing an asterisk in column 7 the line is treated as a comment.

A program consists of four "divisions" which are, in the order they are written:

> IDENTIFICATION DIVISION—describes such information as the program name
>
> ENVIRONMENT DIVISION—describes the the I/O devices and file organizations that the program uses
>
> DATA DIVISION—describes the layouts of the records in the files and declares work space in main store
>
> PROCEDURE DIVISION—contains executable statements.

We will not describe the contents of the IDENTIFICATION and ENVIRONMENT divisions any further as it would divert attention from the essentials of a COBOL program. These two divisions are also a rich source of dialect.

7.3   DATA

The DATA DIVISION begins with the line

> DATA DIVISION.

beginning in the A area. It consists of two sections introduced by the lines:

FILE SECTION.

and

WORKING-STORAGE SECTION.

which again must start in the A area. Everything else in the DATA DIVISION is written in the B area. The FILE SECTION describes the layout of the records in the files that the program processes. The WORKING-STORAGE SECTION declares space for data in main store. The important item of data is the record, which may optionally consists of several components. These components may in turn consist of more simple components, and so on. Thus, records are essentially hierarchical in structure.

The programmer can give records and parts of records names. A name is made up of up to thirty characters, each of which is either a letter or digit (0 to 9), or a hyphen (-). But a name must begin with a letter, and must not end with a hyphen. Unfortunately there are a lot of reserved words in COBOL that cannot be used as names. Worse still, although the standard specifies a list of words, individual systems usually have additional ones which are also taboo. If the programmer does not want or need to give a data item a name he or she can simply use the word FILLER in the data declaration instead of a name.

Returning to the idea of records, suppose we wish to describe a record named DATE that consists of three parts. It can be done as follows:

```
01   DATE
     05  DAY
     05  MONTH
     05  YEAR
```

The number alongside the data names are called level numbers. They indicate how data items are related to each other, as follows. Data items that adjoin each other in a record are described by giving them the same level number. If a data item consists of a collection of more elementary component parts, then they are described by indenting them and giving them a higher level number.

Data items that are not expressed in terms of any more simple components must be described in greater detail. The programmer must state what sort of information the data item is intended to hold and how big it is. Here are some examples:

```
01   PERSON-RECORD.
     05  SALARY        PIC      9(5).
     05  NAME          PIC      A(20).
     05  ADDRESS       PIC      X(40).
     05  TAX-RATE      PIC      9V99.
     05  BANK-BALANCE  PIC S9(4)V99.
```

Here SALARY can be used to accommodate a five digit number, NAME twenty letters and/or spaces, ADDRESS any 40 characters, TAX-RATE a number with two digits after the implied decimal point (indicated by "V"), and BANK-BALANCE a number that can take on negative values (indicated by "S" at the start of the picture). Now that we have written these declarations in full, note that each line ends with a period.

The FILE SECTION of the DATA DIVISION describes the layout of records that are to be input and output. For each file that is to be processed by a program there may be several different record layouts. Each layout must be described as a separate record following the heading FD (for file description) and the file name. These different layouts can be thought of as describing the same area of main store.

The FILE SECTION is used exclusively for describing input or output records. If any other data items are required, for example, to hold a total that is accumulated as a file is processed, then they must be declared in the WORKING-STORAGE SECTION. This part of a program corresponds to an area of main store that is available for use while the program is in execution. It is possible to set up items in WORKING-STORAGE that have fixed values in the following way:

01   TAX-RATE PIC 99   VALUE IS 30.

(The picture and value must correspond.)

Although COBOL freely allows data that has been set up in this way to be modified by the execution of the program, we advise against doing it. Any data item whose value is to change during execution of the program should be initialized only by means of a statement executed in the PROCEDURE DIVISION. This avoids problems should the program be used in a re-entrant manner or if it is to be used as a subprogram that is to be called repeatedly.

Certain useful data items with fixed values do not need to be set up by the programmer because COBOL supplies them. These are ZERO, ZEROES, SPACE and SPACES, with obvious meanings.

7.4   EXECUTABLE STATEMENTS

Statements that cause actions to be carried out when the program is executed are written in the PROCEDURE DIVISION. A COBOL program might typically cause the input of some records of information from a file into the FILE SECTION, some computation on values in the WORKING-STORAGE SECTION, and the output of a formatted report, record by record, from the FILE SECTION.

In general, executable statements can:

(a)   input or output a record to or from the FILE SECTION
(b)   edit or copy information in main store
(c)   carry out calculations
(d)   perform different actions following a test or comparison on data items
(e)   carry out a sequence of these actions. Statements are executed in sequence in the order that they are written, commencing with the first executable statement in the procedure division
(f)   do any of the above repetitively.

Each statement is written starting in the B area and terminated with a period. Execution of the statement

    STOP RUN.

causes the program to terminate with a predefined system message.
    The statement that copies information from one place in main store to another (one data item to another) is the MOVE statement. For example:

    MOVE A TO B.

copies the information in data item named A to data item B. If the two data items involved in a MOVE statement have different pictures, then there are complex rules that stipulate what will happen. We advise that it is safer not to move information to somewhere with a different picture. An exception to this rule arises when it is necessary to deliberately truncate a data item or to edit it.

7.5   SEQUENTIAL INPUT–OUTPUT

    Before an I/O device or file is accessed an OPEN statement must be executed, giving the name of the file (as given in the ENVIRONMENT DIVISION) and stating whether data is to be input from or output to the file. For example:

    OPEN   INPUT TRANSACTION-FILE.
    OPEN   OUTPUT REPORT-FILE.

When a program has ceased using a file it should execute a CLOSE statement. For example:

    CLOSE   TRANSACTION-FILE.

    Information is input and output a complete record at a time using the READ statement. For example:

    READ   TRANSACTION-FILE.
    WRITE   REPORT-LINE.

(This is not completely correct, but it is adequate for the time being.) Notice that with the READ statement the file name is specified, but with the WRITE statement it is the name of one of the records associated with the output file.

When an input record is read, it can be considered to be placed in main store in any one of the descriptions of the records of the file. When there is more than one record description for a file they are like templates that give different layouts to the same area of store.

On output it can be considered that a record is output from the place in main store specified by the record name.

In some dialects of COBOL, records that are to be printed have to be treated specially. The first character of each record must be declared, but not used (it is used by the input–output system to specify vertical line formatting, e.g. skip a page, skip 2 lines then print). Part of a program to input one record and print it looks like this:

```
FD TRANSACTION-FILE.
  01 TRANSACTION-RECORD PIC X(80).

FD REPORT-FILE.
  01 REPORT-LINE.
    05 VERTICAL-FORMAT-CHARACTER PIC X.
    05 COPY-OF-TRANSACTION          PIC X(80).
    05 FILLER                       PIC X(52).

PROCEDURE DIVISION.

PRINT-A-RECORD.
  OPEN INPUT TRANSACTION-FILE
       OUTPUT REPORT-FILE.
  READ TRANSACTION-FILE.
  MOVE SPACES TO REPORT-LINE.
  MOVE TRANSACTION-RECORD TO COPY-OF-TRANSACTION.
  WRITE REPORT-LINE.
  CLOSE TRANSACTION-FILE.
  CLOSE REPORT-FILE.
  STOP RUN.
```

Our explanation of sequential input–output is still incomplete in one important aspect. Since COBOL is primarily a language designed for information processing, the concept of a file is very important. A sequential file is a series of records which can be input one at a time by means of READ statements until the system detects that the end of the file has been reached. When this happens, a special part of the READ statement is executed. A convenient way to write it is shown in the following example:

```
READ TRANSACTION-FILE
  AT END MOVE YES TO END-OF-FILE.
```

where YES and END-OF-FILE are data items declared in WORKING-STORAGE. We describe later how best to process this condition.

7.6 PARAGRAPHS AND THE PERFORM VERB

A long program with many statements may be very hard to understand
if it is written as a single unbroken list of statements. Structured programming helps master such complexity by breaking down problem solutions into
components that can be comprehended. Similarly, the paragraph feature of
COBOL encourages programs to be expressed as a set of (short) sequences
of instructions. Each sequence commences with a paragraph name, starting
in the A margin and ending with a period. (The flexibility of naming is the
same as for data.) The sequence of statements inside a paragraph can be
invoked by executing a PERFORM statement, for example:

    PERFORM PROCESS-FILE.

If PERFORM statements are used the structure of a PROCEDURE DIVISION
typically looks like the following example:

    PROCEDURE DIVISION.

    PROCESS-FILE.
        PERFORM INITIALIZE.
        PERFORM INPUT-AND-PROCESS-RECORDS.
        PERFORM TERMINATE.
        STOP RUN.

    INITIALIZE.
        .
        .
        .

    INPUT-AND-PROCESS-RECORDS.
        .
        .
        .

7.7 REPETITION

A variant of the PERFORM statement can be used to cause a named
paragraph to be executed repeatedly until a condition is met. For example:

    PERFORM SEARCH-TABLE UNTIL ITEM IS EQUAL TO FOUND.

A vitally important thing to remember is that the condition is tested before
the pargraph is executed. One consequence of this is that if the condition is
true to start with, the paragraph will not be executed at all.

As another example, one way of processing a sequential file is to use the
PERFORM statement as follows:

    OPEN INPUT   INPUT-FILE.
    MOVE FALSE TO END-OF-FILE.

```
READ INPUT-FILE AT END
    MOVE TRUE TO END-OF-FILE.
PERFORM READ-AND-PROCESS-RECORD
    UNTIL END-OF-FILE IS EQUAL TO TRUE.
CLOSE INPUT-FILE.
STOP RUN.

READ-AND-PROCESS-RECORD.
    PERFORM PROCESS-RECORD.
    READ INPUT-FILE AT END
        MOVE TRUE TO END-OF-FILE.
```

Note the initial read of the first record, if there is one, for reasons explained in Chapter 3.

The operators available for use in comparisons are as follows. Each can be written in an alternative short way as indicated:

```
IS GREATER THAN          >
IS NOT GREATER THAN   NOT >
IS LESS THAN             <
IS NOT LESS THAN      NOT<
IS EQUAL TO              =
IS NOT EQUAL TO       NOT =
```

Conditions can be combined into more complex expressions using AND and OR operators, and expressions can be negated with the NOT operator. The use of brackets is essential to make such expressions absolutely clear, for example, the program fragment:

```
IF X > Y AND NOT A = B AND C = D
```

is almost incomprehensible. But the following is clearer and unambiguous:

```
IF (X > Y)
   AND
   NOT (A = B AND C = D)
```

The PERFORM... UNTIL construct is vital in situations when the number of repetitions is not known in advance. When the number of iterations is well-defined, however, the PERFORM... TIMES variety of PERFORM statement is useful. Examples are:

```
PERFORM READ-DATA 20 TIMES.

PERFORM ADDITION COUNT TIMES.
```

7.8   COMPARISON

There are three ways of specifying that different actions should be taken as a result of carrying out a test. A simple example of the first way is:

```
IF HOURS-WORKED IS GREATER THAN STANDARD-HOURS
   PERFORM OVERTIME-CALACULATIONS.
```

The conditions that can be tested are the same as those that can be written in the PERFORM... UNTIL statement described above.

In the remainder of this section we choose to use some abysmal data names (short and meaningless) in order to highlight the structures of the IF statement.

In the above example only a single statement, the PERFORM statement, is executed if the condition is met. Alternatively, several statements can be grouped together for execution. For example:

```
IF A IS GREATER THAN B
   MOVE X TO Y
   MOVE P TO Q
   PERFORM PRINT-LINE.
```

Notice that there is one period at the end of the complete IF statement.

A second type of IF statement allows a choice of two different actions to be selected following a comparison:

```
IF HOURS-WORKED IS GREATER THAN STANDARD-HOURS
   PERFORM OVERTIME-CALCULATION
   ADD X TO Y
ELSE
   PERFORM STANDARD-CALCULATION
   ADD P TO Q.
```

Notice again that there is only one period that identifies the end of the complete IF statement. As we explain in Chapter 8, this is a most unfortunate rule. (We also suggest solutions to the problems that arise.)

The logic of an algorithm often decides that IF statements are nested, that is, an IF appears as one of the statements within another IF:

```
IF X IS EQUAL TO Y
   IF P IS EQUAL TO Q
      MOVE X TO Z
ELSE
   MOVE V TO W.
```

We have to be particularly vigilant in this sort of situation because although the sense may be entirely clear to us humans from the indentation, the COBOL compiler instead religiously concentrates only on periods and ELSEs. The rule for understanding nested IF statements is this:

> Examine the program, starting at the top. Whenever an ELSE statement is encountered it matches up with the nearest preceding IF that does not have a corresponding ELSE.

So in the above example, the MOVE V TO W relates to IF P IS EQUAL TO Q.

As we explain in Chapter 8, nesting of IF statements can lead to dangerously unclear coding.

So far we have only described facilities for carrying out at the most two different actions following a test. Sometimes, though, it is necessary to carry out three or more different actions. This third kind of selection can be done using a set of safety nested IF statements, as shown in the following:

```
IF TRANSACTION-TYPE = NEW RECORD
    PERFORM INSERT-NEW-RECORD
ELSE IF TRANSACTION-TYPE = DELETE-RECORD
    PERFORM DELETE-EXISTING-RECORD
ELSE IF TRANSACTION-TYPE = CHANGE-RECORD
    PERFORM UPDATE-RECORD
ELSE
    PERFORM TRANSACTION-ERROR.
```

Although these IF statements are in fact nested to a high degree, they are easy to understand, particularly if the statements are indented as shown.

Sometimes a program has to test data that has been input to see for example whether it does, as intended, consist of digits. COBOL allows this to be done in the following way:

```
IF  D  IS NUMERIC
    .
    .
    .

IF  D  IS NOT NUMERIC
    .
    .
    .
```

Should it be necessary to check to see whether data is alphabetic, we can use statements like this:

```
IF  D  IS ALPHABETIC
    .
    .
    .

IF  D  IS NOT ALPHABETIC
    .
    .
    .
```

As in picture clauses, numeric means the digits 0 to 9 and alphabetic means the letters A to Z and spaces.

Before we leave IF statements, we will indulge in explaining just one feature that, strictly speaking, is superfluous. Consider the following statement:

```
IF SEX IS MALE
    .
    .
    .
```

We can, if we like, write it in the following more compact and possibly more meaningful way:

        IF MALE

        .
        .
        .

In order to do this, however, we have to code an explanation of the "condition" being tested (MALE in this example) immediately after the data to which it refers (SEX in this case), like this:

        01 SEX PIC A.
            88 MALE VALUE IS 'M'.

The level number 88 has this special significance.

7.9 CALCULATION

In COBOL, calculation on data items that have numeric values can be done with the COMPUTE statement. Here is an example:

        COMPUTE NET-PAY = GROSS-PAY − TAX.

The following operators are available:

        +   add
        −   subtract
        *   multiply
        /   divide
        **   raise to the power of

Wherever there is the slightest ambiguity in the meaning of an expression, brackets can and should be used to make the intention clear. (Although there are rules that determine the order of evaluation of any expression, they are easily remembered wrongly, and are a good source of errors.) For example:

        COMPUTE PERCENTAGE-PROFIT
        = (SELL-PRICE − COST-PRICE) / 100.

Expressions inside brackets are always evaluated first. Remember that each operator must be preceded by and followed by at least one space.

        If the data item that is to contain the result of a calculation has a picture that is insufficient to contain the answer, then the result is truncated (or chopped off) so as to fit. For example, if the true answer is 123.456 and the picture is $9(2)V9(2)$ then the actual result will be 23.45. More commonly it is necessary to round an answer, for example, to the nearest whole currency unit. This can be done like this:

```
COMPUTE TAX ROUNDED
    = EARNINGS * TAX-RATE.
```

Although nearly every calculation can be carried out using COMPUTE, there are two other statements that are frequently useful to increment or decrement a count or total. Examples of their use are:

```
ADD ONE TO COUNT.
SUBTRACT SALES FROM STOCK.
```

Very occasionally it may be necessary to compute the remainder that arises from the division of a pair of integers. For this purpose the DIVIDE statement is useful:

```
DIVIDE A BY B GIVING C REMAINDER D.
```

Anyone who has learned COBOL will know that we have chosen not to mention a whole set of verbs that perform calculations. We assert that the facilities we have described are all that are necessary: all else tends to be unnecessary confusion.

7.10   FORMATTING OUTPUT

COBOL is rich in facilities for producing printed output that is attractively laid out. There are two sets of facilities—one for determining where lines are printed on a page and the second for printing numbers in a readable form. The following examples show how lines can be skipped (which is the same as leaving blank lines) and how lines can be printed as a heading at the top of a new page.

```
WRITE REPORT-LINE AFTER ADVANCING 2 LINES.
WRITE HEADING AFTER ADVANCING PAGE.
WRITE SUM BEFORE ADVANCING 1 LINE.
```

To control the layout of a number that is printed, special characters called editing characters are written in the description of the picture of the number. Editing characters allow the printing of:

(a)   the sign,
(b)   the decimal point,
(c)   leading blanks or asterisks,
(d)   a floating currency symbol and/or sign,
(e)   commas, to indicate thousands, millions, etc.

and combinations of these. The rules governing the use of editing characters are complex and it is common to make errors. Here are some examples of the use of editing characters:

value of number	picture	printed text	
023.45	999.99	023.45	
0003.45	ZZZ9.99	3.45	(preceded by 3 blanks)
−02.34	−99.9	−02.3	

Normally numbers are input into the FILE SECTION and calculations are performed in the WORKING-STORAGE SECTION. Then the results are moved to the appropriate part of the FILE SECTION, where their pictures include editing characters, for printing. Calculations cannot then be performed on this edited information.

7.11 TABLES

Much of the information that we have to deal with is presented in the form of tables. Examples are timetables, mathematical tables, and directories. COBOL provides a convenient way of representing such information. The idea is to give every item in a table the same name, and to distinguish an individual item by specifying its position by means of an integer known as a subscript.

Thus, we could declare the following table (in the DATA DIVISION) in order to hold the names of twenty towns:

```
01 TABLE-OF-TOWNS.
   02 TOWN OCCURS 20 PIC X(20).
```

Then the tenth item in the table would be referred to as TOWN (10) and the Tth item (where T is an integer declared in the data division) as TOWN (T).

A variant of the PERFORM verb is useful in processing arrays:

```
PERFORM ADDITION VARYING T
FROM 1 BY 1 UNTIL T = 20.
```

Note that, as with the PERFORM ... UNTIL version of PERFORM, the test is carried out before the paragraph is executed, so the paragraph ADDITION is PERFORMED only 19 times rather than 20.

An element of a table can be either a simple number or a character string. Alternatively each element of a table can be a record or even another table. For example:

```
01 TIME-TABLE.
   02 DESTINATION OCCURS 20.
      03 DESTINATION-NAME PIC X(20).
      03 DEPARTURE-TIME OCCURS 10 PIC 9(4).
```

declares 20 records, each describing a destination. Each record consists of a name and a table of 10 depature times. In the PROCEDURE DIVISION, a reference to:

DESTINATION (6)

means a complete record, the sixth. A reference to:

DEPARTURE-TIME (2, 4)

means the second destination and the fourth time.

One nuisance in COBOL is that it is not easy both to declare a table and give its elements values. For example, we might wish to set up a table containing the names of the days of the week. In order to do it, we first have to declare the data as a record (or some structure other than an array):

```
01 DAYS-OF-WEEK-TEXT.
   02 FILLER PIC A(3) VALUE IS 'MON'.
   02 FILLER PIC A(3) VALUE IS 'TUE'.
   02 FILLER PIC A(3) VALUE IS 'WED'.
   02 FILLER PIC A(3) VALUE IS 'THU'.
   02 FILLER PIC A(3) VALUE IS 'FRI'.
   02 FILLER PIC A(3) VALUE IS 'SAT'.
   02 FILLER PIC A(3) VALUE IS 'SUN'.
```

Then, following this, we code a declaration that describes this same data as a table. This is done using the word REDEFINES as follows:

```
01 DAYS-OF-WEEK REDEFINES DAYS-OF-WEEK-TEXT.
   02 DAY-OF-WEEK PIC A(3) OCCURS 7 TIMES.
```

This declaration asserts that the two items, DAYS-OF-WEEK and DAYS-OF-WEEK-TEXT are one and the same, so that for example DAY-OF-WEEK (3) has the value 'WED'.

7.12 SUBPROGRAMS

As we have seen, the COBOL paragraph facility allows a program to be written as small, manageable parts. One disadvantage of this scheme is that every item in the data division is accessible to every paragraph. This means that if we have a large program and wish to divide the work of writing it amongst several people, then we might have considerable difficulty avoiding clashes of names—both for paragraphs and data. A similar difficulty arises if we wish to create widely useful utility operations for incorporation into a number of different programs.

The COBOL subprogram facility helps solve these problems. A subprogram is written as a completely distinct COBOL program. It has its own IDENTIFICATION, ENVIRONMENT, DATA and PROCEDURE DIVISIONS. It is compiled completely separately and any clashes between names used within it and names used elsewhere do not matter. A subprogram is invoked from a COBOL program or another subprogram by means of a CALL statement. For example:

CALL "UPDATE".

The name of a subprogram is the name that appears in the PROGRAM-ID statement in the IDENTIFICATION DIVISION. (Many implementations of COBOL limit this name to eight characters.) The CALL statement causes execution of the statements within the subprogram just as PERFORM causes execution of the statements within a paragraph. The EXIT PROGRAM statement returns control to the program that invoked the subprogram, at the statement immediately after the CALL. (The EXIT PROGRAM statement must be in a paragraph by itself.)

Invariably data has to be communicated to a subprogram for it to act upon, and results returned to the invoking program. In order to do this:

(a)   The CALL statement specifies the names of data items to be communicated to the subprogram. For example:

CALL "UPDATE" USING TRANSACTION-RECORD, KEY-VALUE.

(b)   In the subprogram, the PROCEDURE DIVISION header mentions the data items that are communicated. For example:

PROCEDURE DIVISION USING X, Y.

The data items must match in order, size and type the information passed to the subprogram by the CALL statement, but the names used need not match up.

(c)   In the subprogram, any data items that appear in the PROCEDURE DIVISION header must be declared in a third part of the DATA DIVISION known as the LINKAGE SECTION.

7.13   SUMMARY

We have described a subset of COBOL that is small but powerful. Our aim has been to indicate how COBOL can be used safely. We have omitted to describe several important facilities provided by the language:

(a)   accessing indexed sequential files
(b)   accessing random access files
(c)   the report-writer feature
(d)   the SORT verb.

Clearly these are valuable, not to say indispensable, features. We suggest that you consult a manual if you want to find out about them.

There are, however, many other COBOL facilities that we have delib-erately chosen not to mention because they accomplish nothing that cannot be achieved using (a collection of) those that we have described. True, "more powerful" features may sometimes allow something to be done in fewer lines of code, but the effort expended by the programmer may be increased as he or she strives to comprehend how to use properly a facility that he or she does not use very often. There is a current school of thought that asserts that programming languages should be small—with a few well-chosen features. We can apply this approach by ignoring much of COBOL.

Our recommendations for using COBOL are:

(a)   use a subset of the language that is clear and can be fully understood
(b)   use nested IF statements carefully. We suggest various ways of doing this in Chapter 8
(c)   use indentation, blank lines, new pages and meaningful names to make programs more readable (see Chapter 9).

7.14   FURTHER READING

1.   Chmura, L. J. and Ledgard, H. F., *COBOL with Style*, Hayden Book Co., Rochelle Park, N.J., 1976.
     This book deals with many of the issues discussed in this chapter.

2.   Kernighan, B. W. and Plauger, P. J., *The Elements of Programming Style*, McGraw-Hill, New York, 1974.
     Again, this book suggests ways of using programming languages more effec-tively. The examples given are in FORTRAN and PL/1.

3.   Anderson, T. and Randell, B. (eds.), *Computing Systems Reliability*, Cambridge University Press, Cambridge, 1979.
     The chapter by J. J. Horning in this book discusses the virtues of using only a subset of a programming language.

7.15   EXERCISE

Investigate the following COBOL facilities and formulate an argument either for or against using them:

(a)   condition names, to make IF statements clearer
(b)   the arithmetic verbs ADD, SUBTRACT, MULTIPLY and DIVIDE
(c)   the report-writer facility for generating a formatted report from a description of its layout
(d)   the STRING, UNSTRING and INSPECT verbs for manipulating strings of characters.

8

Structured
Programming in
COBOL

8.1 INTRODUCTION

In this and Chapter 9 we consider the translation into COBOL of the program design language solutions developed in earlier chapters. We should state immediately that COBOL is *not* the ideal language for structured programming and that more recently designed languages, for example Pascal and Ada, have control structures designed with structured programming specifically in mind. Despite its age, however, COBOL does provide all the essential features we need, albeit sometimes rather clumsily.

The potential advantages gained from adopting a structured approach to coding, in line with the structured approach to program design, far outweigh any difficulties we will encounter due to some inadequacies of COBOL's logic structures. We will show that COBOL does in fact possess each of our three basic logic structures (sequence, selection and repetition), but that their actual form can make structured coding in COBOL in certain situations more awkward than we would like.

To circumvent these problems many installations make successful use of one of a number of COBOL preprocessors which are now widely available. These preprocessors effectively elevate the logic structures of COBOL to those of our program design language. Programmers make use of the enhanced logic structures which are then translated into standard COBOL by the preprocessor. In this chapter we assume the programmer has access only to a reasonable COBOL compiler.

The main objectives of these chapters are to show:

(a) how programs designed using pseudocode can be readily converted into COBOL code
(b) that structured coding in COBOL is a practical and profitable proposition.

This chapter discusses the issues concerning the implementation of our basic logic structures in COBOL, while Chapter 9 shows how these may then be used to translate the program designs developed in Chapters 3, 5 and 6.

8.2 SEQUENCE

Sequence simply means that statements are to be executed in the order or sequence in which they are written. This structure is basic to nearly all programming languages; in COBOL it simply means that source statements are executed in the sequence in which they appear within the source code. An example is:

```
MOVE 0 TO ACCOUNT-TOTAL
           SALESMAN-TOTAL
           REGION-TOTAL
           FINAL-TOTAL.
MOVE ACCOUNT-NUMBER TO PREVIOUS-ACCOUNT-NUMBER.
MOVE SALESMAN-NUMBER TO PREVIOUS-SALESMAN-NUMBER.
MOVE REGION-NUMBER TO PREVIOUS-REGION-NUMBER.
MOVE 1 TO LINE-NUMBER.
MOVE 1 TO PAGE-NUMBER.
```

Some pseudocode sequences will contain references to modules which are fully elaborated at a lower level of a program design. Generally in COBOL these will be represented by a call to PERFORM the paragraph containing the code of the module.

For example, consider the following top-level decomposition for a report generation problem and its COBOL equivalent.

PDL	COBOL
report program	REPORT-PROGRAM.
initialization	PERFORM INITIALIZATION.
generate report	PERFORM GENERATE-REPORT.
termination	PERFORM TERMINATION.
halt execution	STOP RUN.

A PERFORM statement requires the named paragraph to be executed and has the same effect as if PERFORM were replaced by the COBOL code of the named procedure and each statement in that code were to be executed in sequence. Alternatively some modules may warrant implementation as separate subprograms in COBOL and would then be invoked by a CALL statement to the subprogram.

8.3 REPETITION

The **perform . . . until** construct used in our program design language is implemented directly in COBOL. The syntax of a simple PERFORM ...UNTIL statement in COBOL is as follows:

> PERFORM paragraph name
> UNTIL condition.

We should remember that, somewhat surprisingly, the terminating condition is tested at the beginning of the loop and hence we have the, often useful, possibility that the specified paragraph may never be executed if the condition is initially true.

COBOL's PERFORM . . . UNTIL statement presently does not allow in-line coding. The body of the loop controlled by a PERFORM statement must be placed in a separate program module. Future enhancements to COBOL can be expected to provide an in-line looping mechanism. Two other forms of COBOL's PERFORM statement are often useful. If a paragraph is to be executed a certain known number of times, the TIMES clause may be used as follows:

> PERFORM paragraph name integer TIMES.

If indexing or subscript manipulation with tables is required or a counter is to be incremented on each iteration of a loop, the variation of PERFORM using the VARYING, FROM and BY clauses should be used. For example:

> PERFORM READ-VALUES-INTO-TABLE
>   VARYING TABLE-SUB
>   FROM 1 BY 1 UNTIL TABLE-SUB > TABLE-LENGTH.

8.4 SELECTION

In the simplest of cases our program design language construct

> **if** condition
> **then**
>   statement(s)
> **else**
>   statement(s)
> **endif**

transforms directly into an equivalent COBOL IF statement. COBOL IF statements have the following syntax:

```
IF condition
    {statements-1 or
    NEXT SENTENCE}
ELSE
    {statements-2 or
    NEXT SENTENCE}.
```

There are a number of points to be made. First the keyword **then** does not appear in ANS COBOL although it is included as an optional extension in many implementations. Secondly the keyword **endif** used as a terminator in our program design language, is replaced in COBOL by a period. Also, the **else** clause is optional and null or empty statement sequences may be denoted using the NEXT SENTENCE clause.

<table>
<tr><td align="center">PDL</td><td align="center">COBOL</td></tr>
<tr><td>

if consumption more than 100 units
then
    customer is on special tariff
else
    customer is on normal tariff
endif

</td><td>

```
IF CONSUMPTION > 100
    MOVE 'S' TO TARIFF
ELSE
    MOVE 'N' TO TARIFF.
```

</td></tr>
</table>

The COBOL comment facility (an '*' in column 7) may be used to effect an even greater correspondence between PDL and COBOL code:

```
    IF CONSUMPTION > 100
*       THEN
            MOVE 'S' TO TARIFF
        ELSE
            MOVE 'N' TO TARIFF.
*       ENDIF
```

8.5 NESTED IF STATEMENTS

In the program design language solutions developed in Chapters 3, 4 and 6 we saw that the use of nested **if** statements is an important part of structured program design. Before the advent of structured programming, many COBOL installations actively discouraged the use of nested IF statements for two main reasons.

Firstly, they were said to be difficult to understand. A number of research experiments have shown this to be the case when nesting is any more than a few levels deep. We would recommend the use of nested IF statements but, as suggested in the chapter on program design, two should be the maximum level of nesting.

Secondly, nested IF statements were said to be less efficient than equivalent code written using only simple one-level IF and GO TO statements. This argument has its foundation in the fact that many COBOL compilers generate far from optimal machine language code for nested IF statements, which subsequently slows the execution of the program. Whilst a saving of a few microseconds at run-time may be achieved, most COBOL practitioners now agree that this benefit is far overshadowed by the loss of readability and maintainability which occurs as a result. In many installations the same inefficient code argument was used to discourage the use of the PERFORM statement in favor of the GO TO statement. A discussion on the use of the GO TO statement appears in section 8.7.

In order to correctly implement nested conditional structures we must understand that there is a major difference between the use by COBOL of the period as a terminator for conditional statements and the way in which we used the **endif** keyword for the same purpose in our PDL. The effect of **endif** was to terminate the scope of *only* the most recent **if** lacking an **endif**. The effect of the COBOL period, however, is to terminate *all* previously unclosed IFs.

In many cases nested conditional structures from our PDL may be translated into COBOL without concern for the differing effect of the respective terminators. Consider the following example:

PDL	COBOL
if condition	IF condition
then	IF condition
if condition	statement(s)
then	ELSE
statement(s)	statement(s)
else	ELSE
statement(s)	statement(s).
endif	
else	
statement(s)	
endif	

However, some pseudocode sequences do not have a direct implementation in COBOL. For example, suppose we wish to translate the following structure.

```
if condition – A
then
  if condition – B
  then
    statement(s)
  endif
else
  statement(s)
endif
```

A direct translation would give:

```
IF condition – A
  IF condition – B
    statement(s)
  ELSE
    statement(s).
```

This is syntactically correct COBOL but its effect is different from that of our PDL statements. The problem arises because of the lack of an **endif** operator in COBOL. Since we cannot insert a period at the end of the inner IF statement (this would terminate both the inner and the outer IF statements), there is now ambiguity as to which IF statement ELSE is paired with.

COBOL overcomes this ambiguity with a specific rule: ELSE is paired with the most recent IF statement without a corresponding ELSE. Following this rule we can see that the ELSE statement in our example is paired with the inner IF statement. Do not be hoodwinked into thinking otherwise by the indentation used.

However, a simple solution is at hand. Notice that the problem would be resolved if we inserted a null or "do nothing" ELSE statement for the inner IF. The NEXT SENTENCE clause in COBOL accomplishes this.

```
IF condition – A
  IF condition – B
    statement(s)
  ELSE
    NEXT SENTENCE
ELSE
  statement(s).
```

The possibility of IF . . . ELSE mismatches can be removed by adopting the simple rule that every IF must have a matching ELSE. All null ELSE statements should therefore be coded using the NEXT SENTENCE clause. This rule is often relaxed to allow the removal of null ELSE statements at the end of a nested IF statement. However, there is a valid reason to retain even these seemingly redundant trailing ELSE...NEXT SENTENCE statements as they are often a valuable aid in identifying subtle logic errors which might otherwise be troublesome to find. For example, in the following code fragment suppose that the statement

ADD 1 TO SALES-DEPARTMENT-COUNT

was intended to be included within the scope of the IF statement:

```
IF DEPARTMENT-CODE = "SALES"
    MOVE "SALES DEPARTMENT" TO DEPARTMENT-MESSAGE.
    ADD 1 TO SALES-DEPARTMENT-COUNT.
```

The inclusion of a trailing ELSE ... NEXT SENTENCE clause (see below) will allow the COBOL compiler to draw our attention to the erroneous inclusion of the period after the MOVE statement.

```
IF DEPARTMENT-CODE = "SALES"
    MOVE "SALES DEPARTMENT" TO DEPARTMENT-MESSAGE.
    ADD 1 TO SALES-DEPARTMENT-COUNT
ELSE
    NEXT SENTENCE.
```

The offending period will terminate the IF statement, leading the compiler to reject the following ELSE as having no matching IF statement.

A second problem which may occur during translation of IF statements is illustrated by the following example and its direct implementation in COBOL.

PDL	COBOL
if condition−A	IF condition−A
then	
if condition−B	IF condition−B
then	
statements−1	statements−1
else	ELSE
statements−2	statements−2
endif	
statements−3	statements−3
else	ELSE
statements−4	statements−4.
endif	

Here the problem is that statements−3 is associated with the ELSE of the inner IF statement, whereas in the pseudocode it is independent of the inner **if**. Again the difficulty is caused by the fact that the COBOL period terminates all unclosed IF statements as opposed to only the most recent one as with our pseudocode **endif**.

The simplest and most general solution to the problem is to PERFORM, the inner IF statement. That is, extract the inner IF from the outer IF into a separate paragraph which can then be performed. The COBOL becomes:

```
IF condition−A
    PERFORM INNER-IF
    statements−3
ELSE
    statements−4.

INNER-IF.
    IF condition−B
        statements−1
    ELSE
        statements−2.
```

This has the disadvantage of being less efficient. But more importantly, by moving the inner IF "out of line" the correspondence between the pseudocode and matching COBOL code is no longer immediately clear.

In some cases it may be possible to adopt alternative solutions which do not have these drawbacks. For example, it may be possible to simply relocate statements−3 before the inner IF, provided the effect of the logic remains unchanged:

```
IF condition−A
    statements−3
    IF condition−B
        statements−1
    ELSE
        statements−2
ELSE
    statements−4.
```

Alternatively if *statements−3* consists of only a small number of COBOL statements it might be preferable, at the expense of introducing inefficiency due to repeated code, to include them within both the true and false actions of the inner IF, thus removing the drawback of "out of line" code. The COBOL code becomes:

```
IF condition−A
    IF condition−B
        statements−1
        statements−3
    ELSE
        statements−2
        statements−3
ELSE
    statements−4.
```

The IF statement is not alone in its use of the period as a terminator. For example, the period in COBOL is often used to block together actions which are to be associated with an exception condition such as an "end of file" condition or an "invalid key" error when processing a file. Another example is the use of the ON SIZE ERROR clause in an arithmetic statement to deal with the possibility of arithmetic overflow in a result field. Consider the examples below.

```
READ OLD-MASTER-FILE
   AT END MOVE HIGH-VALUES TO OLD-MASTER KEY.

WRITE INDEXED-FILE
   INVALID KEY
      MOVE 1 TO UPDATE-ERROR-FOUND
      MOVE "INVALID ADDITION" TO UPDATE-ERROR-MESSAGE.

COMPUTE GROSS-SALARY = (REGULAR-HOURS + (1.5 *
   OVERTIME-HOURS)) * HOURLY-PAY-RATE
   ON SIZE ERROR
      DISPLAY "GROSS SALARY OVERFLOW"
      MOVE "TRUE" TO OVERFLOW-ERROR.
```

It should be clear that we must be extremely careful when using such statements within IF statements as the period required to terminate the exception condition actions will also terminate any unclosed IF statements. The most general solution is again to use PERFORM, to execute a paragraph which will contain the offending statement.

8.6 THE CASE STATEMENT

The **case** statement in our program design language extended the idea of selection to enable the selection for execution of one action from a set of many alternative actions. It is a multi-way branch structure where the conditions involved are mutually exclusive and based on the value of a single data variable.

For example, the pseudocode for a simple validate or edit program might contain the following:

```
case transaction type of
   addition        :  validate addition
   deletion        :  validate deletion
   change name     :  validate change name
   change address  :  validate change address
   else            :  transaction type error
endcase
```

There is no **case** statement as such in COBOL but we will consider two ways in which it may be simulated.

Alternative 1

If the single data variable on which the selection is to be based (transaction type in our example) can only take values in the range 1 up to some maximum integer value then the **case** structure may be simulated using a combination of the PERFORM, GO TO... DEPENDING ON, and GO TO statements.

If we suppose in our example that transaction type takes values 1, 2, 3 and 4 respectively then our example could be written as below:

```
        .
        .
        .
PERFORM VALIDATE-TRANSACTION
    THRU VALIDATE-TRANSACTION-EXIT.
        .
        .
        .

VALIDATE-TRANSACTION.
    GO TO
        VALIDATE-ADDITION
        VALIDATE-DELETION
        VALIDATE-CHANGE-OF-NAME
        VALIDATE-CHANGE-OF-ADDRESS
    DEPENDING ON TRANSACTION-TYPE.
    GO TO TRANSACTION-TYPE-ERROR.

VALIDATE-ADDITION.
        .
        .
    GO TO VALIDATE-TRANSACTION-EXIT.

VALIDATE-DELETION.
        .
        .
    GO TO VALIDATE-TRANSACTION-EXIT.

VALIDATE-CHANGE-OF-NAME.
        .
        .
    GO TO VALIDATE-TRANSACTION-EXIT.

VALIDATE-CHANGE-OF-ADDRESS.
        .
        .
    GO TO VALIDATE-TRANSACTION-EXIT.

TRANSACTION-TYPE-ERROR.
        .
        .
```

```
GO TO VALIDATE-TRANSACTION-EXIT.

VALIDATE-TRANSACTION-EXIT.
    EXIT.
```

The GO TO . . . DEPENDING ON statement tests the value of the single data variable, in this case TRANSACTION-TYPE, and branches to the first paragraph in the list of supplied paragraph names if the value is 1, the second if the value is 2 etc. If the value is outside the range 1 to the number of paragraphs listed then no branch is made. Therefore, in our example if TRANSACTION-TYPE is invalid (not 1, 2, 3 or 4) then control passes through to the GO TO TRANSACTION-TYPE-ERROR statement which allows handling of the invalid transaction type.

The GO TO VALIDATE-TRANSACTION-EXIT statements included as the very last statement in each of the alternative paragraphs ensure that one and only one of the alternative actions will be executed.

The one entry–one exit structure is preserved by invoking the **case** structure using a PERFORM . . . THRU . . . statement.

We cannot help but notice that this simulation is achieved through heavy use of the normally much frowned upon GO TO statement. We believe that the use of the GO TO in a very controlled manner to construct a well-structured logic structure is perfectly acceptable. A fuller discussion of how to make appropriate use of the GO TO is given in a later section of this chapter.

Alternative 2

The simplest method of implementing the **case** structure in COBOL is to replace the GO TO . . . DEPENDING ON statement with a chained series of IF statements as:

```
IF TRANSACTION-TYPE = 1
    PERFORM VALIDATE-ADDITION
ELSE IF TRANSACTION-TYPE = 2
    PERFORM VALIDATE-DELETION
ELSE IF TRANSACTION-TYPE = 3
    PERFORM VALIDATE-CHANGE-OF-NAME
ELSE IF TRANSACTION-TYPE = 4
    PERFORM VALIDATE-CHANGE-OF-ADDRESS
ELSE
    PERFORM TRANSACTION-TYPE-ERROR.
```

Notice that the normal indentation rules for nested IF statements are adjusted to reflect the fact that the IF statements are *not* nested but simply chained together. Also, chained IF statements do not present the same understandability problems as nested IF statements and, therefore, we place no limit on the number of IF statements that may be chained together in this manner.

Comparing our two alternative simulations, the most important consideration is that the GO TO... DEPENDING ON representation is severely limited by the fact that the dependent variable has to take values in the range 1 up to some maximum. In many cases this will render this method unusable.

The chained IF statement is a truly general method and is capable of handling the case for example where our different TRANSACTION-TYPEs were signified by non-numeric values such as "ADD", "DEL", "CNM" and "CAD".

8.7   THE GO TO STATEMENT

Much of the early debate concerning structured programming revolved around the issue of whether or not the GO TO or unconditional branch statement should be used. Many COBOL programmers equated structured programming with GO TO-less programming and felt understandably threatened when one of their principal program building tools was so heavily attacked.

Should we use the GO TO statement in COBOL? Yes. The question we should answer is, "in what circumstances is it the most appropriate structure to use?" It is the undisciplined use of the GO TO statement, producing incomprehensible programs that structured programming attempts to control.

Developing our programs using the basic structures of sequence, selection and repetition will result in programs with few, if any, GO TO statements. However, there are some situations where the controlled use of the GO TO will actually improve program understandability.

Sometimes the GO TO can be used to avoid some inadequacy of the programming language we are using. We have already seen that one of the most efficient implementations of the **case** statement, that is missing in COBOL, involved the controlled use of the GO TO. In a similar way we could even write programs in an assembly language by simulating our ideal logic structures using the primitives of the low-level language.

We should not use the GO TO to avoid some inadequacy of our program design. When such a problem occurs it is often extremely tempting to adopt a "quick and dirty" fix by patching up the code with a few GO TO statements here and there. Do not! Go back to the program design and, as suggested earlier, trace the cause of the design fault and amend the design and eventually the program code accordingly.

Situations in which the use of a GO TO will improve program understandability are rare. But one of the more common situations arises when we wish to exit from a module prematurely because of the occurrence of some condition. Examples are an arithmetic operation overflow or a key sequence error when processing a file. The standard technique for handling such a situation would be to set a flag which would allow a premature exit through the normal exit point of the module. In the example below we wish to recognise the failure of a simple linear table search to find a requested table entry.

```
FIND-EMPLOYEE.
    SET EMPLOYEE-INDEX TO 1.
    MOVE "MATCH POSSIBLE" TO EMPLOYEE-ERROR-FLAG.
    SEARCH EMPLOYEE-TABLE
        AT END MOVE "NO MATCH" TO EMPLOYEE-ERROR-FLAG
        WHEN   REQUESTED-EMPLOYEE-NUMBER = EMPLOYEE-NUMBER
        (EMPLOYEE-INDEX)
            MOVE EMPLOYEE-NUMBER (EMPLOYEE-INDEX) TO
            REQUESTED-EMPLOYEE-NAME.
    IF EMPLOYEE-ERROR-FLAG NOT = "NO MATCH"
    . . .
```

Sometimes this technique can lead to somewhat clumsy code. Imagine the situation where such an "exception" condition occurs within a module nested several levels deep within our program structure. In such a case resumption of normal processing may be impossible and it may be necessary to output some appropriate message and abort the job. To achieve a "clean" exit from our program using our flag technique we would need to include conditional logic to cause exits from each level of our program structure as we move towards the highest levels. This solution tends to get out of control if we have not one, but a number of such exception conditions handled in a similar way. Possibly the most understandable way of dealing with this situation is to allow a branch to an error handling routine which will abort the job.

Both of the examples we have discussed have involved *forward branches* to achieve an exit from a routine. There is little justification for *backward* branching; we already have a construct for creating repetition structures.

In conclusion, the GO TO statement should be used only after carefully considering whether its use is justified on the grounds of improving the quality of our program in some way or whether we are using it to hide some defect in our program design.

8.8 PROGRAM MODULES

Throughout the earlier chapters of the book we have stressed the importance of constructing designs which have highly cohesive and loosely coupled components. In this section we consider how these design attributes are supported by COBOL.

When coded in COBOL a component in a design will correspond to either a paragraph or a subprogram. The subprogram has a distinct advantage over the paragraph as an implementation vehicle. Subprograms enable far greater control over data references than paragraphs do: a paragraph in a program module potentially has access to all data items within that module, thus all the paragraphs in a program module share access to a common data environment; the DATA DIVISION of that module. On the other hand, communication between subprograms is limited to data items expressly listed in a parameter list. All other data items in a subprogram are inaccessible to all other subprograms. COBOL, therefore, provides data control facilities at the subprogram level but not at the paragraph level. Paragraphs within a COBOL program module are therefore potentially strongly coupled to each other and the onus is on the programmer to exercise control over data references. Such control becomes almost impossible if a large program is constructed as a single monolithic COBOL program with many hundreds of paragraphs and data items. Clearly, solely on the grounds of ensuring that access to data items remains under control, the use of subprograms is to be recommended. The programs found in this text are small compared with the program systems of many thousands of lines of code commonly found in data processing installations. Such programs can only be constructed by teams of programmers who develop a partitioned system of separately implemented, compiled and tested subprogram modules loosely coupled to one another.

Finally, earlier in this section we mentioned only the paragraph and the subprogram as possible implementation structures for design components. The omission of the COBOL section was intentional: a section allows the programmer to group together a collection of related paragraphs under a section name which can be invoked in the same manner as a paragraph using a PERFORM statement. Used in this way, the section is a one entry, one exit structure. However, COBOL provides no control to prevent individual paragraphs within a section from being invoked from outside the section. A section, therefore, potentially has multiple entry and exit points and, for this reason, we do not recommend its use.

8.9 SUMMARY

In this chapter we have discussed the implementation in COBOL of the logic structures of our program design language.

COBOL is not the most suitable language for structured programming. In particular, nested IF statements can give rise to problems. But with care structured COBOL programs are practical and have been developed successfully for many years by many programming installations. Most importantly a good correspondence can be achieved between the structure of the COBOL code and the structure of the program design.

COBOL has control structures for sequence, selection and repetition, although in some situations these control structures are less than adequate. The problem situations have been identified and methods for overcoming these shortcomings have been suggested.

The use of the GO TO statement has been advocated to avoid language inadequacies but not design inadequacies.

The advantages of the subprogram over the paragraph for the implementation of program design components were discussed. Large programs should be partitioned into separately compiled subprograms.

We can expect future ANSI standard versions of COBOL to remedy many of the problems outlined in this chapter by including in the language such features as an in-line repetition structure, a CASE statement and an ENDIF terminator for IF statements.

9

Coding in COBOL

9.1 INTRODUCTION

In earlier chapters we have traced in detail the design of three typical programs—a program to print a report, a program to validate (or check) input data, and a program to update a sequential file. These design efforts led to the production of an algorithm for each program, expressed in pseudocode. In the belief that the only way to master COBOL is to completely understand only a part of it, we presented in Chapter 7 a description of a useful subset of COBOL. Chapter 8 went on to explore the ways in which a program design expressed in pseudocode can be translated into COBOL coding that retains the structure of the design. In this chapter, after examining some suggestions for good coding practice, we show the COBOL coding for the three program examples designed earlier.

A first consideration for good coding concerns names. COBOL is bountiful in allowing data and paragraph names to be long; it allows the programmer to choose meaningful names, rather than names that suffer from cryptic abbreviation. It is easy, though, to commit the error of using meaningful names which are similar to one another—leading to confusion. Names should be meaningful, but diverse. Some psychological experiments suggest that it is clearer if names differ at their beginnings rather than at their endings. For example, we should use:

WOMEN-COUNT and MEN-COUNT

rather than

COUNT-OF-WOMEN and COUNT-OF-MEN.

144

In some organizations the programming standards dictate that data names should begin with the prefix I-, O-, or W-, depending on whether they are input, output or WORKING-STORAGE SECTION items. It seems to us that this is a poor substitute for a cross-reference listing (specifying where things are declared and used) produced automatically by the compiler or some other utility. The same may be true of conventions for the prefixes on paragraph names that are sometimes insisted upon.

As for level numbers in the DATA DIVISION, some organizations insist that they are coded at intervals of 2 (or sometimes 5) as follows:

```
01 RECORD-NAME
   03 FIRST-COMPONENT
   03 SECOND
      05 PART-OF-SECOND
      05 ETCETERA
```

The reason for doing this is to ease the later insertion of new level numbers in between the existing ones.

What we would wholeheartedly recommend is paying attention to the layout of programs. It helps readability enormously to indent the appropriate parts of record declarations, the body of IF statements and the ends of statements that are too long for a single line.

Paragraphs that carry out related functions can be grouped next to each other in the program text, so that they can easily be studied together. Perhaps the single most useful aid to reading is to place a group of related paragraphs (or indeed a single critical paragraph) on a page by itself so that it can be studied without the distraction of other code. What should certainly be avoided is allowing a paragraph to spill over from one page to another. Such a crime makes understanding of the code near impossible.

One most contentious suggestion is that, if the above coding rules are followed, few (if any) comments are necessary. If names of paragraphs accurately describe what they do, if the names of data clearly convey what they are, and if paragraphs are short (see Chapter 4) and carry out well-defined activities then the intent of a program is clear without additional text. Indeed, since amendments to comments are rarely pursued as conscientiously as changes to code, many programs contain comments that are actually misleading—worse than useless.

To see the end products of this preaching, read on.

9.2 REPORT PROGRAM

In this section we present the monthly sales summary report program for the Nu-wave Cosmetic Co. problem of Chapter 3. The program presented implements the algorithm detailed in section 3.5. Notice that there is one-to-one correspondence between components of the program design and paragraphs in the resulting COBOL program.

```
DATA DIVISION.

FILE SECTION.

FD   SALES-FILE
     LABEL RECORDS OMITTED.

01   SALES-RECORD.
     05 TERRITORY                    PIC 99.
     05 AREA-CODE                    PIC 9.
     05 SALESPERSON-NUMBER           PIC 9(5).
     05 SALESPERSON-NAME             PIC X(30).
     05 SALES-AMOUNT                 PIC 9(5)V99.


FD   SALES-SUMMARY-FILE
     LABEL RECORDS OMITTED.

01   SALES-SUMMARY-RECORD            PIC X(133).

WORKING-STORAGE SECTION.

01   FLAGS.
     05 SALES-FILE-END-FLAG          PIC X(5).
        88 END-OF-SALES-FILE-REACHED  VALUE "TRUE".

01   SAVE-ITEMS.
     05 PREVIOUS-TERRITORY           PIC 99.
     05 PREVIOUS-AREA-CODE           PIC 9.
     05 PREVIOUS-SALESPERSON-NUMBER PIC 9(5).
     05 PREVIOUS-SALESPERSON-NAME    PIC X(30).
     05 NUMBER-OF-TERRITORIES        PIC 99.
     05 PAGE-COUNT                   PIC 999.
     05 LINE-SKIP-COUNT              PIC 999.

01   TOTALS.
     05 GRAND-TOTAL                  PIC 9(8)V99.
     05 TERRITORY-TOTAL              PIC 9(8)V99.
     05 AREA-TOTAL                   PIC 9(8)V99.
     05 SALESPERSON-TOTAL            PIC 9(8)V99.


01   TERRITORY-TABLE.
     05 TERRITORY-SALES-TOTALS OCCURS 1 TO 20 TIMES
            DEPENDING ON NUMBER-OF-TERRITORIES
            INDEXED BY TERRITORY-INDEX.
        10 TERRITORY-CODE            PIC 99.
        10 TERRITORY-TOTALS          PIC 9(8)V99.
```

```
*****************************************************************
*              REPORT LINE LAYOUT DETAILS                      *
*****************************************************************


01  REPORT-HEADING-LINE-1.
    05 FILLER                        PIC X(56) VALUE SPACES.
    05 FILLER                        PIC X(22)
              VALUE "NU-WAVE COSMETICS".
    05 FILLER                        PIC X(55) VALUE SPACES.


01  REPORT-HEADING-LINE-2.
    05 FILLER                        PIC X(53) VALUE SPACES.
    05 FILLER                        PIC X(28)
              VALUE "MONTHLY SALES SUMMARY REPORT".
    05 FILLER                        PIC X(37) VALUE SPACES.
    05 FILLER                        PIC X(5) VALUE "PAGE ".
    05 PAGE-COUNT-OUT                PIC ZZ9.
    05 FILLER                        PIC X(5) VALUE SPACES.


01  AREA-SUMMARY-HEADING-LINE.
    05 FILLER                        PIC X(11) VALUE SPACES.
    05 FILLER                        PIC X(10) VALUE "TERRITORY ".
    05 TERRITORY-ASH                 PIC 99.
    05 FILLER                        PIC X(90) VALUE SPACES.
    05 FILLER                        PIC X(5) VALUE "AREA ".
    05 AREA-ASH                      PIC 9.
    05 FILLER                        PIC X(14) VALUE SPACES.


01  AREA-SUMMARY-COLUMN-HEADING.
    05 FILLER                        PIC X(41) VALUE SPACES.
    05 FILLER                        PIC X(11) VALUE "SALESPERSON".
    05 FILLER                        PIC X(38) VALUE SPACES.
    05 FILLER                        PIC X(24)
              VALUE "MONTHLY SALES AMOUNT ($)".
    05 FILLER                        PIC X(9) VALUE SPACES.



01  SALESPERSON-DETAIL-LINE.
    05 FILLER                        PIC X(11) VALUE SPACES.
    05 SALESPERSON-NUMBER-OUT        PIC 9(5).
    05 FILLER                        PIC X(10) VALUE SPACES.
    05 SALESPERSON-NAME-OUT          PIC X(30).
    05 FILLER                        PIC X(42) VALUE SPACES.
    05 SALESPERSON-TOTAL-OUT         PIC Z(8)9.99.
    05 FILLER                        PIC X(11) VALUE SPACES.


01  AREA-TOTAL-LINE.
    05 FILLER                        PIC X(71) VALUE SPACES.
    05 FILLER                        PIC X(12)
                          VALUE " AREA TOTAL".
    05 FILLER                        PIC X(5) VALUE SPACES.
    05 AREA-TOTAL-OUT                PIC $(8)9.99.
    05 FILLER                        PIC X(32) VALUE SPACES.
```

```
01  TERRITORY-SUMMARY-DETAIL-LINE.
    05 FILLER                      PIC X(51) VALUE SPACES.
    05 TERRITORY-SUMMARY-CODE      PIC Z9.
    05 FILLER                      PIC X(8) VALUE SPACES.
    05 TERRITORY-SUMMARY-TOTAL     PIC Z(8)9.99.
    05 FILLER                      PIC X(61) VALUE SPACES.

01  TERRITORY-SUMMARY-HEADING.
    05 FILLER                      PIC X(46) VALUE SPACES.
    05 FILLER                      PIC X(9) VALUE "TERRITORY".
    05 FILLER                      PIC X(13) VALUE SPACES.
    05 FILLER                      PIC X(9) VALUE "SALES ($)".
    05 FILLER                      PIC X(56) VALUE SPACES.

01  GRAND-TOTAL-LINE.
    05 FILLER                      PIC X(55) VALUE SPACES.
    05 FILLER                      PIC X(19)
       VALUE "TOTAL MONTHLY SALES".
    05 GRAND-TOTAL-OUT             PIC $(8)9.99.
    05 FILLER                      PIC X(54) VALUE SPACES.


**************************************************************
*               TOP LEVEL ROUTINES                          *
**************************************************************

 PROCEDURE DIVISION.

 PRODUCE-SALES-SUMMARY-REPORT.
     PERFORM INITIALIZATION.
     IF NOT END-OF-SALES-FILE-REACHED
         PERFORM EXTRACT-SUMMARY-INFORMATION
         PERFORM PRINT-TERRITORY-SUMMARY
     ELSE
         DISPLAY "EMPTY SALES FILE ENCOUNTERED".
     PERFORM TERMINATION.
     STOP RUN.

 INITIALIZATION.
     OPEN INPUT SALES-FILE
          OUTPUT SALES-SUMMARY-FILE
     MOVE "FALSE" TO SALES-FILE-END-FLAG.
     PERFORM READ-SALES-RECORD.
     IF NOT END-OF-SALES-FILE-REACHED
         MOVE ZERO TO SALESPERSON-TOTAL
                      AREA-TOTAL
                      TERRITORY-TOTAL
                      GRAND-TOTAL
         MOVE SALESPERSON-NUMBER TO PREVIOUS-SALESPERSON-NUMBER
         MOVE SALESPERSON-NAME TO PREVIOUS-SALESPERSON-NAME
         MOVE AREA-CODE TO PREVIOUS-AREA-CODE
         MOVE TERRITORY TO PREVIOUS-TERRITORY
         SET TERRITORY-INDEX TO 1
         MOVE ZERO TO NUMBER-OF-TERRITORIES
         MOVE 1 TO PAGE-COUNT
         PERFORM PRINT-AREA-SUMMARY-HEADINGS.
```

```
EXTRACT-SUMMARY-INFORMATION.
        PERFORM PROCESS-EACH-SALES-RECORD
            UNTIL END-OF-SALES-FILE-REACHED.
        PERFORM PROCESS-FINAL-CONTROL-BREAK.



PRINT-TERRITORY-SUMMARY.
      PERFORM PRINT-TERRITORY-HEADINGS.
      PERFORM PRINT-TERRITORY-SALES-SUMMARY
        VARYING TERRITORY-INDEX FROM 1 BY 1
            UNTIL TERRITORY-INDEX > NUMBER-OF-TERRITORIES.
      PERFORM PRINT-GRAND-TOTAL-LINE.



TERMINATION.
      CLOSE SALES-FILE
            SALES-SUMMARY-FILE.



*********************************************************************
*            CONTROL BREAK PROCESSING ROUTINES                     *
*********************************************************************

PROCESS-EACH-SALES-RECORD.
      IF TERRITORY NOT = PREVIOUS-TERRITORY
          PERFORM PROCESS-A-TERRITORY-BREAK
      ELSE IF AREA-CODE NOT = PREVIOUS-AREA-CODE
                PERFORM PROCESS-AN-AREA-BREAK
            ELSE IF SALESPERSON-NUMBER NOT =
                      PREVIOUS-SALESPERSON-NUMBER
                PERFORM PROCESS-A-SALESPERSON-BREAK.
      ADD SALES-AMOUNT TO SALESPERSON-TOTAL
                          AREA-TOTAL
                          TERRITORY-TOTAL
                          GRAND-TOTAL.
      PERFORM READ-SALES-RECORD.



PROCESS-FINAL-CONTROL-BREAK.
        PERFORM PROCESS-A-TERRITORY-BREAK.



PROCESS-A-TERRITORY-BREAK.
      PERFORM PROCESS-AN-AREA-BREAK.
      ADD 1 TO NUMBER-OF-TERRITORIES.
      MOVE TERRITORY-TOTAL TO TERRITORY-TOTALS (TERRITORY-INDEX).
      MOVE PREVIOUS-TERRITORY TO TERRITORY-CODE (TERRITORY-INDEX).
      SET TERRITORY-INDEX UP BY 1.
      MOVE TERRITORY TO PREVIOUS-TERRITORY.
      MOVE 0 TO TERRITORY-TOTAL.
```

```
PROCESS-AN-AREA-BREAK.
      PERFORM PROCESS-A-SALESPERSON-BREAK.
      PERFORM PROCESS-END-OF-AREA-SUMMARY.
      MOVE AREA-CODE   TO
                  PREVIOUS-AREA-CODE.
      MOVE 0 TO AREA-TOTAL.



  PROCESS-END-OF-AREA-SUMMARY.
      MOVE AREA-TOTAL TO AREA-TOTAL-OUT.
      MOVE 5 TO LINE-SKIP-COUNT.
      MOVE AREA-TOTAL-LINE TO SALES-SUMMARY-RECORD.
      PERFORM PRINT-AREA-SUMMARY-REPORT-LINE.
      IF NOT END-OF-SALES-FILE-REACHED
          PERFORM PRINT-AREA-SUMMARY-HEADINGS.



  PROCESS-A-SALESPERSON-BREAK.
      MOVE PREVIOUS-SALESPERSON-NUMBER TO
          SALESPERSON-NUMBER-OUT.
      MOVE PREVIOUS-SALESPERSON-NAME TO SALESPERSON-NAME-OUT.
      MOVE SALESPERSON-TOTAL TO SALESPERSON-TOTAL-OUT.
      MOVE 1 TO LINE-SKIP-COUNT.
      MOVE SALESPERSON-DETAIL-LINE TO SALES-SUMMARY-RECORD.
      PERFORM PRINT-AREA-SUMMARY-REPORT-LINE.
      MOVE SALESPERSON-NUMBER TO
                  PREVIOUS-SALESPERSON-NUMBER.
      MOVE SALESPERSON-NAME TO PREVIOUS-SALESPERSON-NAME.
      MOVE 0 TO SALESPERSON-TOTAL.



****************************************************************
*              INPUT FILE PROCESSING ROUTINES               *
****************************************************************

  READ-SALES-RECORD.
      READ SALES-FILE
          AT END MOVE "TRUE" TO SALES-FILE-END-FLAG.


****************************************************************
*              AREA SUMMARY REPORT PRINT ROUTINES           *
****************************************************************

  PRINT-AREA-SUMMARY-HEADINGS.
      PERFORM PRINT-REPORT-HEADINGS.
      MOVE TERRITORY TO TERRITORY-ASH.
      MOVE AREA-CODE TO AREA-ASH.
      WRITE SALES-SUMMARY-RECORD FROM AREA-SUMMARY-HEADING-LINE
          AFTER ADVANCING 3 LINES.
      WRITE SALES-SUMMARY-RECORD FROM AREA-SUMMARY-COLUMN-HEADING
          AFTER ADVANCING 3 LINES.
```

```
PRINT-AREA-SUMMARY-REPORT-LINE.
     WRITE SALES-SUMMARY-RECORD
         AFTER ADVANCING LINE-SKIP-COUNT LINES.


************************************************************
*      TERRITORY SUMMARY REPORT PRINT ROUTINES            *
************************************************************


PRINT-TERRITORY-SALES-SUMMARY.
     MOVE TERRITORY-CODE (TERRITORY-INDEX) TO
         TERRITORY-SUMMARY-CODE.
     MOVE TERRITORY-TOTALS (TERRITORY-INDEX)
         TO TERRITORY-SUMMARY-TOTAL.
     MOVE 1 TO LINE-SKIP-COUNT.
     MOVE TERRITORY-SUMMARY-DETAIL-LINE TO SALES-SUMMARY-RECORD.
     PERFORM PRINT-TERRITORY-SUMMARY-LINE.


 PRINT-GRAND-TOTAL-LINE.
     MOVE GRAND-TOTAL TO GRAND-TOTAL-OUT.
     MOVE GRAND-TOTAL-LINE TO SALES-SUMMARY-RECORD.
     MOVE 4 TO LINE-SKIP-COUNT.
     PERFORM PRINT-TERRITORY-SUMMARY-LINE.


 PRINT-TERRITORY-HEADINGS.
     PERFORM PRINT-REPORT-HEADINGS.
     WRITE SALES-SUMMARY-RECORD FROM TERRITORY-SUMMARY-HEADING
         AFTER ADVANCING 3 LINES.


 PRINT-TERRITORY-SUMMARY-LINE.
     WRITE SALES-SUMMARY-RECORD
         AFTER ADVANCING LINE-SKIP-COUNT LINES.


************************************************************
*          REPORT HEADING PRINT ROUTINE(S)               *
************************************************************


 PRINT-REPORT-HEADINGS.
     MOVE PAGE-COUNT  TO PAGE-COUNT-OUT.
     WRITE SALES-SUMMARY-RECORD FROM REPORT-HEADING-LINE-1
         AFTER ADVANCING PAGE.
     WRITE SALES-SUMMARY-RECORD FROM REPORT-HEADING-LINE-2
         AFTER ADVANCING 3 LINES.
     ADD 1 TO PAGE-COUNT.


************************************************************
*          END OF PROGRAM                                 *
************************************************************
```

9.3 VALIDATE PROGRAM

We present here the coding of the validate program for the gas billing system designed in Chapter 5. The coding arises directly from the design. We have chosen to implement the pseudocode **case** construction in the design using a GO TO ... DEPENDING ON statement rather than using the alternative of "chained" IF statements.

```
DATA DIVISION.

FILE SECTION.

FD  CARDS
    LABEL RECORDS ARE OMITTED.

01  INPUT-TRANSACTION.
    05  TRANSACTION-CODE      PIC 9.
    05  REFERENCE-NUMBER.
        10  FILLER           PIC 9(4).
        10  CHECK-DIGITS      PIC 99.
    05  FILLER               PIC X(73).

01  METER-READING.
    05  FILLER               PIC 9.
    05  FILLER               PIC 9(6).
    05  METER-READING-FIELD  PIC 9(5).
    05  FILLER               PIC X(68).

01  CUSTOMER-PAYMENT.
    05  FILLER               PIC 9.
    05  FILLER               PIC 9(6).
    05  PAYMENT-AMOUNT        PIC 9(4)V99.
    05  FILLER               PIC X(67).

01  ADJUST-METER-NUMBER.
    05  FILLER               PIC 9.
    05  FILLER               PIC 9(6).
    05  NEW-METER-NUMBER      PIC 9(6).
    05  FILLER               PIC X(67).

01  ADJUST-NAME.
    05  FILLER               PIC 9.
    05  FILLER               PIC 9(6).
    05  ADJUSTED-NAME         PIC X(20).
    05  FILLER               PIC X(53).

01  NEW-CUSTOMER-1.
    05  FILLER               PIC 9.
    05  FILLER               PIC 9(6).
    05  CUSTOMER-NAME         PIC X(20).
    05  ADDRESS-LINE-1        PIC X(20).
    05  ADDRESS-LINE-2        PIC X(20).
    05  FILLER               PIC X(13).
```

```
01  NEW-CUSTOMER-2.
    05  FILLER             PIC 9.
    05  FILLER             PIC 9(6).
    05  METER-NUMBER       PIC 9(6).
    05  READING-DATE       PIC 99.
    05  PREVIOUS-INDEX     PIC 9(5).
    05  TARIFF             PIC A.
    05  SPECIAL-INS        PIC X(15).
    05  CONSUMPTION        PIC 9(5).
    05  AMOUNT-DUE         PIC 9(4)V99.
    05  DATE-FIELD         PIC 9(6).
    05  B-F-BALANCE        PIC S9(4)V99.
    05  FILLER             PIC X(21).


FD  TRANSACTIONS
    LABEL RECORDS ARE STANDARD.

01  OUTPUT-TRANSACTION     PIC X(80).

FD  ERROR-REPORT
    LABEL RECORDS ARE OMITTED.

01  HEADING-LINE.
    05  FILLER             PIC X.
    05  FILLER             PIC X(19).
    05  HEADING-TEXT       PIC X(12).
    05  FILLER             PIC X(101).

01  TRANSACTION-LINE.
    05  FILLER             PIC X.
    05  TRANSACTION-TEXT   PIC X(80).
    05  FILLER             PIC X(52).

01  ERROR-LINE.
    05  FILLER             PIC X.
    05  FILLER             PIC X(5).
    05  ERROR-TEXT         PIC X(50).
    05  FILLER             PIC X(77).

01  FOOTING-LINE.
    05  FILLER             PIC X.
    05  TOTAL-ERRORS       PIC 9(5).
    05  FOOTING-TEXT       PIC X(17).
    05  FILLER             PIC X(110).


WORKING-STORAGE SECTION.

01  NEXT-TRANSACTION.
    03  NEXT-TRAN-STATUS       PIC X.
    03  NEXT-TRAN-DETAILS.
        05  NEXT-TRAN-CODE     PIC X.
        05  NEXT-TRAN-REF      PIC X(6).
        05  FILLER             PIC X(73).
    03  NEXT-ERRORS.
        05  NEXT-ERROR         PIC X OCCURS 21.
```

```
01  CURRENT-TRANSACTION.
    03  CURRENT-TRAN-STATUS        PIC X.
    03  CURRENT-TRAN-DETAILS.
        05  CURRENT-TRAN-CODE      PIC X.
        05  CURRENT-TRAN-REF       PIC X(6).
        05  FILLER                 PIC X(73).
    03  CURRENT-ERRORS.
        05  CURRENT-ERROR          PIC X OCCURS 21.

01  PREVIOUS-TRANSACTION.
    03  PREVIOUS-TRAN-STATUS       PIC X.
    03  PREVIOUS-TRAN-DETAILS.
        05  PREVIOUS-TRAN-CODE     PIC X.
        05  PREVIOUS-TRAN-REF      PIC X(6).
        05  FILLER                 PIC X(73).
    03  PREVIOUS-ERRORS.
        05  PREVIOUS-ERROR         PIC X OCCURS 21.

01  FLAGS.
    03  DOES-EXIST                 PIC X VALUE "Y".
    03  DOES-NOT-EXIST             PIC X VALUE "N".
    03  END-OF-FILE                PIC X.

01  ERROR-CONTROL.
    03  ERROR-NUMBER               PIC 99.
    03  ERROR-COUNT                PIC 9(5).
    03  NO-ERRORS                  PIC X(21)
            VALUE IS "NNNNNNNNNNNNNNNNNNNNN".
    03  CHECK                      PIC 99.

01  REPORT-TEXT.
    03  REPORT-HEADING             PIC X(12)
            VALUE IS "ERROR REPORT".
    03  REPORT-FOOTING             PIC X(17)
            VALUE IS " ERRORS DETECTED".

01  ERROR-MESSAGES-TEXT.
    05 M1  PIC X(50) VALUE IS "TRANSACTION CODE INVALID".
    05 M2  PIC X(50) VALUE IS "REFERENCE NUMBER INVALID".
    05 M3  PIC X(50) VALUE IS "METER READING INVALID".
    05 M4  PIC X(50) VALUE IS "PAYMENT AMOUNT INVALID".
    05 M5  PIC X(50) VALUE IS "NEW METER NUMBER INVALID".
    05 M6  PIC X(50) VALUE IS "ADJUSTED NAME INVALID".
    05 M7  PIC X(50) VALUE IS "CUSTOMER NAME INVALID".
    05 M8  PIC X(50) VALUE IS "ADDRESS INVALID".
    05 M9  PIC X(50) VALUE IS "REFERENCE NOS DIFFERENT".
    05 M10 PIC X(50) VALUE IS "METER NUMBER INVALID".
    05 M11 PIC X(50) VALUE IS "READING DATE INVALID".
    05 M12 PIC X(50) VALUE IS "PREVIOUS INDEX INVALID".
    05 M13 PIC X(50) VALUE IS "TARIFF INVALID".
    05 M14 PIC X(50) VALUE IS "CONSUMPTION INVALID".
    05 M15 PIC X(50) VALUE IS "AMOUNT DUE INVALID".
    05 M16 PIC X(50) VALUE IS "DATE INVALID".
    05 M17 PIC X(50) VALUE IS "B/F BALANCE INVALID".
    05 M18 PIC X(50) VALUE IS "6 NOT FOLLOWED BY 7".
    05 M19 PIC X(50) VALUE IS "7 PRECEDED BY INVALID 6".
    05 M20 PIC X(50) VALUE IS "6 FOLLOWED BY INVALID 7".
    05 M21 PIC X(50) VALUE IS "7 NOT PRECEDED BY 6".
```

```
01  ERROR-MESSAGES REDEFINES ERROR-MESSAGES-TEXT.
    05  ERROR-MESSAGE      PIC X(50) OCCURS 21 TIMES.


***********************************************************************
*            START OF PROGRAM                                         *
***********************************************************************


PROCEDURE DIVISION.

VALIDATE.
    PERFORM INITIALIZE.
    PERFORM CHECK-TRANSACTION UNTIL END-OF-FILE = "Y".
    PERFORM COMPLETE-PROCESSING.
    STOP RUN.

CHECK-TRANSACTION.
    PERFORM CHECK-NEXT-TRANSACTION
        THRU CHECK-NEXT-TRANSACTION-EXIT.
    PERFORM CHECK-DEPENDENCIES-OF-CURRENT.
    PERFORM DISPATCH-PREVIOUS-TRANSACTION.
    MOVE CURRENT-TRANSACTION TO PREVIOUS-TRANSACTION.
    MOVE NEXT-TRANSACTION TO CURRENT-TRANSACTION.
    MOVE SPACES TO NEXT-TRANSACTION.
    MOVE NO-ERRORS TO NEXT-ERRORS.
    PERFORM READ-TRANSACTION.



DISPATCH-PREVIOUS-TRANSACTION.
    IF PREVIOUS-TRAN-STATUS = DOES-EXIST
        IF PREVIOUS-ERRORS NOT = NO-ERRORS
            PERFORM PRINT-TRANSACTION
            PERFORM PRINT-ERRORS
        ELSE
            PERFORM WRITE-TRANSACTION-TO-FILE.



***********************************************************************
*            INITIALIZATION AND TERMINATION                           *
***********************************************************************


INITIALIZE.
    OPEN INPUT CARDS.
    OPEN OUTPUT TRANSACTIONS.
    OPEN OUTPUT ERROR-REPORT.
    MOVE NO-ERRORS TO NEXT-ERRORS.
    MOVE ZEROES TO ERROR-COUNT.
    MOVE SPACES TO HEADING-LINE.
    MOVE REPORT-HEADING TO HEADING-TEXT.
    WRITE HEADING-LINE AFTER ADVANCING TO-NEW-PAGE.
    MOVE "N" TO END-OF-FILE.
    PERFORM READ-TRANSACTION.
    MOVE DOES-NOT-EXIST TO CURRENT-TRAN-STATUS.
    MOVE DOES-NOT-EXIST TO PREVIOUS-TRAN-STATUS.
```

```
COMPLETE-PROCESSING.
      MOVE SPACES TO FOOTING-LINE.
      MOVE DOES-NOT-EXIST TO NEXT-TRAN-STATUS.
      PERFORM CHECK-DEPENDENCIES-OF-CURRENT.
      PERFORM DISPATCH-PREVIOUS-TRANSACTION.
      MOVE CURRENT-TRANSACTION TO PREVIOUS-TRANSACTION.
      PERFORM DISPATCH-PREVIOUS-TRANSACTION.
      MOVE SPACES TO FOOTING-LINE.
      MOVE ERROR-COUNT TO TOTAL-ERRORS.
      MOVE REPORT-FOOTING TO FOOTING-TEXT.
      WRITE FOOTING-LINE AFTER ADVANCING 4 LINES.
      CLOSE CARDS.
      CLOSE TRANSACTIONS.
      CLOSE ERROR-REPORT.



**************************************************************
*              SWITCH ON TRANSACTION NUMBER                  *
**************************************************************

   CHECK-NEXT-TRANSACTION.
      GO TO
            CHECK-TYPE1
            CHECK-TYPE2
            CHECK-TYPE3
            CHECK-TYPE4
            CHECK-TYPE5
            CHECK-TYPE6
            CHECK-TYPE7
      DEPENDING ON TRANSACTION-CODE.
            MOVE "Y" TO NEXT-ERROR (1).
            GO TO CHECK-NEXT-TRANSACTION-EXIT.

   CHECK-TYPE1.
      PERFORM CHECK-REFERENCE-NUMBER.
      PERFORM CHECK-METER-READING.
      GO TO CHECK-NEXT-TRANSACTION-EXIT.

   CHECK-TYPE2.
      PERFORM CHECK-REFERENCE-NUMBER.
      PERFORM CHECK-PAYMENT-AMOUNT.
      GO TO CHECK-NEXT-TRANSACTION-EXIT.

   CHECK-TYPE3.
      PERFORM CHECK-REFERENCE-NUMBER.
      PERFORM CHECK-NEW-METER-NUMBER.
      GO TO CHECK-NEXT-TRANSACTION-EXIT.

   CHECK-TYPE4.
      PERFORM CHECK-REFERENCE-NUMBER.
      PERFORM CHECK-ADJUSTED-NAME.
      GO TO CHECK-NEXT-TRANSACTION-EXIT.
```

```
CHECK-TYPE5.
    PERFORM CHECK-REFERENCE-NUMBER.
    GO TO CHECK-NEXT-TRANSACTION-EXIT.


CHECK-TYPE6.
    PERFORM CHECK-REFERENCE-NUMBER.
    PERFORM CHECK-CUSTOMER-NAME.
    PERFORM CHECK-ADDRESS.
    GO TO CHECK-NEXT-TRANSACTION-EXIT.


CHECK-TYPE7.
    PERFORM CHECK-REFERENCE-NUMBER.
    PERFORM CHECK-METER-NUMBER.
    PERFORM CHECK-READING-DATE.
    PERFORM CHECK-PREVIOUS-INDEX.
    PERFORM CHECK-TARIFF.
    PERFORM CHECK-CONSUMPTION.
    PERFORM CHECK-AMOUNT-DUE.
    PERFORM CHECK-DATE.
    PERFORM CHECK-B-F-BALANCE.
    GO TO CHECK-NEXT-TRANSACTION-EXIT.


CHECK-NEXT-TRANSACTION-EXIT.
    EXIT.




***************************************************************
*         CHECK INTERDEPENDENCIES BETWEEN TRANSACTIONS        *
***************************************************************


CHECK-DEPENDENCIES-OF-CURRENT.
    IF CURRENT-TRAN-STATUS = DOES-EXIST
        IF CURRENT-TRAN-CODE = 6
            PERFORM CHECK-INTERDEPENDENCIES-OF-6
        ELSE
            IF CURRENT-TRAN-CODE = 7
                PERFORM CHECK-INTERDEPENDENCIES-OF-7.




CHECK-INTERDEPENDENCIES-OF-6.
    IF NEXT-TRAN-CODE = 7
        IF NEXT-ERRORS NOT = NO-ERRORS
            MOVE "Y" TO CURRENT-ERROR (20)
        ELSE
            NEXT SENTENCE
    ELSE
        MOVE "Y" TO CURRENT-ERROR (18).
```

```
CHECK-INTERDEPENDENCIES-OF-7.
    IF PREVIOUS-TRAN-CODE = 6
        PERFORM COMPARE-REFERENCE-NUMBERS
        IF PREVIOUS-ERRORS NOT = NO-ERRORS
            MOVE "Y" TO CURRENT-ERROR (19)
        ELSE
            NEXT SENTENCE
    ELSE
        MOVE "Y" TO CURRENT-ERROR (21).
```

```
**********************************************************************
*                 INPUT AND OUTPUT                                   *
**********************************************************************
```

```
READ-TRANSACTION.
    READ CARDS AT END MOVE "Y" TO END-OF-FILE.
    IF END-OF-FILE = "N"
        MOVE DOES-EXIST TO NEXT-TRAN-STATUS
        MOVE INPUT-TRANSACTION TO NEXT-TRAN-DETAILS.
```

```
PRINT-ERRORS.
    PERFORM LOOK-FOR-ERROR
        VARYING ERROR-NUMBER
        FROM 1 BY 1 UNTIL ERROR-NUMBER = 22.
    ADD 1 TO ERROR-COUNT.
```

```
LOOK-FOR-ERROR.
    IF PREVIOUS-ERROR (ERROR-NUMBER) = "Y"
        MOVE SPACES TO ERROR-LINE
        MOVE ERROR-MESSAGE (ERROR-NUMBER) TO ERROR-TEXT
        WRITE ERROR-LINE AFTER ADVANCING 1 LINES.
```

```
PRINT-TRANSACTION.
    MOVE SPACES TO TRANSACTION-LINE.
    MOVE PREVIOUS-TRAN-DETAILS TO TRANSACTION-TEXT.
    WRITE TRANSACTION-LINE AFTER ADVANCING 2 LINES.
```

```
WRITE-TRANSACTION-TO-FILE.
    MOVE PREVIOUS-TRAN-DETAILS TO OUTPUT-TRANSACTION.
    WRITE OUTPUT-TRANSACTION.
```

```
*********************************************************************
*                 DETAILED CHECKING OF FIELDS                      *
*********************************************************************


CHECK-REFERENCE-NUMBER.
    IF REFERENCE-NUMBER IS NOT NUMERIC
        MOVE "Y" TO NEXT-ERROR (2)
    ELSE
        IF REFERENCE-NUMBER IS < 010000
            OR
            REFERENCE-NUMBER IS > 020000
            MOVE "Y" TO NEXT-ERROR (2).


CHECK-METER-READING.
    IF METER-READING-FIELD IS NOT NUMERIC
        MOVE "Y" TO NEXT-ERROR (3).


CHECK-PAYMENT-AMOUNT.
    IF PAYMENT-AMOUNT IS NOT NUMERIC
        MOVE "Y" TO NEXT-ERROR (4)
    ELSE
        IF PAYMENT-AMOUNT IS EQUAL TO 0
            MOVE "Y" TO NEXT-ERROR (4).


CHECK-NEW-METER-NUMBER.
    IF NEW-METER-NUMBER IS NOT NUMERIC
        MOVE "Y" TO NEXT-ERROR (5).


CHECK-ADJUSTED-NAME.
    IF ADJUSTED-NAME IS EQUAL TO SPACES
        MOVE "Y" TO NEXT-ERROR (6).


CHECK-CUSTOMER-NAME.
    IF  CUSTOMER-NAME = SPACES
        MOVE "Y" TO NEXT-ERROR (7).


CHECK-ADDRESS.
    IF ADDRESS-LINE-1 IS EQUAL TO SPACES
        OR
        ADDRESS-LINE-2 IS EQUAL TO SPACES
        MOVE "Y" TO NEXT-ERROR (8).


COMPARE-REFERENCE-NUMBERS.
    IF CURRENT-TRAN-REF
        NOT =
        PREVIOUS-TRAN-REF
        MOVE "Y" TO CURRENT-ERROR (9)
        MOVE "Y" TO PREVIOUS-ERROR (9).


CHECK-METER-NUMBER.
    IF METER-NUMBER IS NOT NUMERIC
        MOVE "Y" TO NEXT-ERROR (10).
```

```
CHECK-READING-DATE.
    IF  READING-DATE IS NOT NUMERIC
        MOVE "Y" TO NEXT-ERROR (11)
    ELSE
        IF READING-DATE IS < 2 OR > 28
            MOVE "Y" TO NEXT-ERROR (11)
        ELSE
            ADD 10 READING-DATE GIVING CHECK
            IF CHECK NOT = CHECK-DIGITS
                MOVE "Y" TO NEXT-ERROR (11).


CHECK-PREVIOUS-INDEX.
    IF PREVIOUS-INDEX IS NOT NUMERIC
        MOVE "Y" TO NEXT-ERROR (12).


CHECK-TARIFF.
    IF TARIFF IS NOT EQUAL TO "S"
        AND
        TARIFF IS NOT EQUAL TO "N"
        MOVE "Y" TO NEXT-ERROR (13).


CHECK-CONSUMPTION.
    IF  CONSUMPTION IS NOT NUMERIC
        AND
        CONSUMPTION IS NOT EQUAL TO SPACES
        MOVE "Y" TO NEXT-ERROR (14).


CHECK-AMOUNT-DUE.
    IF AMOUNT-DUE IS NOT NUMERIC
        AND
        AMOUNT-DUE IS NOT = SPACES
        MOVE "Y" TO NEXT-ERROR (15).


CHECK-DATE.
    IF DATE-FIELD IS NOT NUMERIC
        AND
        DATE-FIELD IS NOT = SPACES
        MOVE "Y" TO NEXT-ERROR (16).


CHECK-B-F-BALANCE.
    IF B-F-BALANCE IS NOT NUMERIC
        AND
        B-F-BALANCE IS NOT = SPACES
        MOVE "Y" TO NEXT-ERROR (17).


****************************************************************
*           END OF PROGRAM                                    *
****************************************************************
```

9.4 SEQUENTIAL FILE UPDATE PROGRAM

In this section we present the COBOL sequential file update program for the telephone company problem of Chapter 6. The program presented implements the algorithm detailed in Section 6.7. Those components dealing with the creation and processing of monthly activity records for billing purposes are implemented as stubs. Rather than recording details of each call made by a customer in the monthly activity record, only a record of the total cost of all calls made is registered in the billing record. Also, the update log report simply lists all rejected transactions with a message detailing why each was rejected. No detailed report formatting is included.

The algorithm described in Chapter 6 makes use of the concept of a sentinel value; whenever the end of a file is reached on either the transactions or master file the read routine is to return a sentinel value greater than any valid key value. It is important that this should be implemented such that all valid key values are allowed. In particular, *low-values* and *high-values* for alphanumeric fields and all zero and all nine for numeric fields may be valid key values and should not then be chosen as sentinel values. To ensure that there will always be a suitable sentinel value, the logical key can be constructed by extending the physical key with an additional first byte. If we ensure that for all valid key values this additional byte is set to, say, zero for numeric keys then a sentinel value can be achieved by moving all nines to the complete logical key.

For example, in the telephone company problem the field phone number is the physical key field for the transaction file:

```
05 TRANSACTION-PHONE-NUMBER        PIC 9(10).
```

The logical key is then defined as:

```
05 TRANSACTION-KEY.
   10 FILLER                        PIC 9 VALUE ZERO.
   10 TRANSACTION-PHYSICAL-KEY      PIC 9(10).
```

and a suitable Sentinel key is

```
05 SENTINEL-KEY                     PIC 9(11)
                              VALUE 99999999999.
```

The input component for the transactions file is then defined as:

```
READ-A-TRANSACTION.
   READ ACCOUNTS-TRANSACTION-FILE
      AT END MOVE SENTINEL-KEY TO TRANSACTION-KEY.
   IF TRANSACTION-KEY NOT = SENTINEL-KEY
      MOVE TRANSACTION-PHONE-NUMBER TO
      TRANSACTION-PHYSICAL-KEY.
```

```
DATA DIVISION.

FILE SECTION.

FD   OLD-CUSTOMER-MASTER-FILE
     LABEL RECORDS ARE OMITTED.

01   OLD-CUSTOMER-RECORD.
     05 OLD-CUSTOMER-PHONE-NUMBER       PIC 9(10).
     05 OLD-CUSTOMER-NAME               PIC X(30).
     05 OLD-CUSTOMER-BILLING-ADDRESS    PIC X(60).
     05 OLD-BASIC-MONTHLY-CHARGE        PIC 9(4)V99.
     05 OLD-ACCOUNT-BALANCE             PIC S9(6)V99.


FD   NEW-CUSTOMER-MASTER-FILE
     LABEL RECORDS ARE OMITTED.

01   NEW-CUSTOMER-RECORD               PIC X(114).


FD   ACCOUNTS-TRANSACTION-FILE
     LABEL RECORDS ARE OMITTED.

01   ACCOUNTS-TRANSACTION-RECORD.
     05 TRANSACTION-PHONE-NUMBER       PIC 9(10).
     05 TRANSACTION-SERIAL-NUMBER      PIC 9(9).
     05 TRANSACTION-TYPE               PIC X.
     05 TRANSACTION-DETAILS.
        10 INSERTION-DETAILS.
           15 INSERTION-NAME           PIC X(30).
           15 INSERTION-ADDRESS        PIC X(60).
           15 INSERTION-MONTHLY-CHARGE PIC 9(4)V99.

        10 DELETION-DETAILS REDEFINES INSERTION-DETAILS.
           15 DELETION-DATE            PIC 9(6).
           15 FILLER                   PIC X(90).

        10 PAYMENT-DETAILS REDEFINES INSERTION-DETAILS.
           15 PAYMENT-AMOUNT           PIC S9(6)V99.
           15 PAYMENT-DATE             PIC 9(6).
           15 FILLER                   PIC X(82).

        10 PHONE-CALL-DETAILS REDEFINES INSERTION-DETAILS.
           15 PHONE-NUMBER-CALLED      PIC 9(10).
           15 PHONE-CALL-DATE          PIC 9(6).
           15 PHONE-CALL-DURATION      PIC 9(4).
           15 PHONE-CALL-COST          PIC 9(4)V99.
           15 FILLER                   PIC X(70).


FD   BILLING-FILE
     LABEL RECORDS ARE OMITTED.
```

```
01  BILLING-RECORD.
    05 BILLING-PHONE-NUMBER          PIC 9(10).
    05 BILLING-CUSTOMER-NAME         PIC X(30).
    05 BILLING-CUSTOMER-ADDRESS      PIC X(60).
    05 BILLING-MONTHLY-CHARGE        PIC 9(4)V99.
    05 BILLING-OPENING-BALANCE       PIC S9(6)V99.
    05 BILLING-COST-OF-CALLS-MADE    PIC 9(6)V99.
    05 BILLING-PAYMENTS-MADE         PIC S9(6)V99.
    05 BILLING-TAX-ADDED             PIC 9(6)V99.
    05 BILLING-CLOSING-BALANCE       PIC S9(6)V99.


FD  UPDATE-LOG-REPORT
    LABEL RECORDS ARE OMITTED.


01  UPDATE-LOG-RECORD                PIC X(133).


FD  CLOSED-ACCOUNT-FILE
    LABEL RECORDS ARE OMITTED.


01  CLOSED-ACCOUNT-RECORD.
    05 CLOSED-PHONE-NUMBER           PIC 9(10).
    05 CLOSED-CUSTOMER-NAME          PIC X(30).
    05 CLOSED-CUSTOMER-ADDRESS       PIC X(60).
    05 CLOSED-DATE                   PIC 9(6).
    05 CLOSED-FINAL-BALANCE          PIC S9(6)V99.


WORKING-STORAGE SECTION.

01  MASTER-CUSTOMER-RECORD.
    05 MASTER-CUSTOMER-PHONE-NUMBER     PIC 9(10).
    05 MASTER-CUSTOMER-NAME             PIC X(30).
    05 MASTER-CUSTOMER-ADDRESS          PIC X(60).
    05 MASTER-BASIC-MONTHLY-CHARGE      PIC 9(4)V99.
    05 MASTER-ACCOUNT-BALANCE           PIC S9(6)V99.

01  KEYS.
    05 TRANSACTION-KEY.
       10 FILLER                       PIC 9 VALUE ZERO.
       10 TRANSACTION-PHYSICAL-KEY      PIC 9(10).

    05 OLD-MASTER-KEY.
       10 FILLER                       PIC 9 VALUE ZERO.
       10 OLD-MASTER-PHYSICAL-KEY       PIC 9(10).

    05 CURRENT-MASTER-KEY               PIC 9(11).
    05 SENTINEL-KEY                     PIC 9(11)
             VALUE 99999999999.
```

```
01  KEY-STATUS-DETAILS.
    05 STATUS-OF-CURRENT-KEY          PIC 9.
    05 ALLOCATED                      PIC 9 VALUE 1.
    05 UNALLOCATED                    PIC 9 VALUE 0.

01  BILLING-DETAILS.
    05 TAX-RATE                       PIC 99V99 VALUE 7.00.

01  UPDATE-LOG-TRANSACTION-LINE.
    05 FILLER                         PIC X(5) VALUE SPACES.
    05 UPDATE-LOG-TRANSACTION         PIC X(116).

01  UPDATE-LOG-ERROR-LINE.
    05 FILLER                         PIC X(5) VALUE SPACES.
    05 UPDATE-LOG-MESSAGE             PIC X(128).


****************************************************************
*            MAIN PROGRAM                                      *
****************************************************************

PROCEDURE DIVISION.

UPDATE-MASTER-FILE.
    PERFORM OPEN-FILES.
    PERFORM READ-A-TRANSACTION.
    PERFORM READ-AN-OLD-MASTER.
    PERFORM CHOOSE-NEXT-KEY-TO-PROCESS.
    PERFORM PROCESS-SEQUENCE-ON-NEXT-KEY
       UNTIL CURRENT-MASTER-KEY = SENTINEL-KEY.
    PERFORM CLOSE-FILES.
    STOP RUN.


****************************************************************
*          KEY AND INPUT FILE PROCESSING ROUTINES             *
****************************************************************

OPEN-FILES.
    OPEN INPUT OLD-CUSTOMER-MASTER-FILE
               ACCOUNTS-TRANSACTION-FILE
         OUTPUT
               UPDATE-LOG-REPORT
               NEW-CUSTOMER-MASTER-FILE
               CLOSED-ACCOUNT-FILE
               BILLING-FILE.



READ-A-TRANSACTION.
    READ ACCOUNTS-TRANSACTION-FILE
       AT END MOVE SENTINEL-KEY TO TRANSACTION-KEY.
    IF TRANSACTION-KEY NOT = SENTINEL-KEY
       MOVE TRANSACTION-PHONE-NUMBER TO TRANSACTION-PHYSICAL-KEY.
```

```
READ-AN-OLD-MASTER.
    READ OLD-CUSTOMER-MASTER-FILE
        AT END MOVE SENTINEL-KEY TO OLD-MASTER-KEY.
    IF OLD-MASTER-KEY NOT = SENTINEL-KEY
        MOVE OLD-CUSTOMER-PHONE-NUMBER TO OLD-MASTER-PHYSICAL-KEY.


CHOOSE-NEXT-KEY-TO-PROCESS.
    IF TRANSACTION-KEY < OLD-MASTER-KEY
        MOVE TRANSACTION-KEY TO CURRENT-MASTER-KEY
    ELSE
        MOVE OLD-MASTER-KEY TO CURRENT-MASTER-KEY.


PROCESS-SEQUENCE-ON-NEXT-KEY.
    PERFORM INITIATE-KEY-PROCESSING.
    PERFORM PROCESS-A-TRANSACTION
        UNTIL TRANSACTION-KEY NOT = CURRENT-MASTER-KEY.
    PERFORM TERMINATE-KEY-PROCESSING.
    PERFORM CHOOSE-NEXT-KEY-TO-PROCESS.


CLOSE-FILES.
    CLOSE OLD-CUSTOMER-MASTER-FILE
          NEW-CUSTOMER-MASTER-FILE
          BILLING-FILE
          ACCOUNTS-TRANSACTION-FILE
          UPDATE-LOG-REPORT
          CLOSED-ACCOUNT-FILE.


INITIATE-KEY-PROCESSING.
    IF OLD-MASTER-KEY = CURRENT-MASTER-KEY
        MOVE OLD-CUSTOMER-RECORD TO MASTER-CUSTOMER-RECORD
        MOVE ALLOCATED TO STATUS-OF-CURRENT-KEY
        PERFORM CREATE-BILLING-ACTIVITY-RECORD
        PERFORM READ-AN-OLD-MASTER
    ELSE
        MOVE UNALLOCATED TO STATUS-OF-CURRENT-KEY.


PROCESS-A-TRANSACTION.
    PERFORM APPLY-TRANSACTION-TO-MASTER.
    PERFORM READ-A-TRANSACTION.


TERMINATE-KEY-PROCESSING.
    IF STATUS-OF-CURRENT-KEY = ALLOCATED
        PERFORM CALCULATE-FINAL-BALANCE
        MOVE BILLING-CLOSING-BALANCE TO MASTER-ACCOUNT-BALANCE
        PERFORM SEND-ACCOUNT-TO-BILLING-FILE
        WRITE NEW-CUSTOMER-RECORD FROM MASTER-CUSTOMER-RECORD.
```

```
****************************************************************
*                TRANSACTION PROCESSING ROUTINES              *
****************************************************************
APPLY-TRANSACTION-TO-MASTER.
    IF TRANSACTION-TYPE = "I"
        PERFORM PROCESS-INSERTION
    ELSE IF TRANSACTION-TYPE = "D"
        PERFORM PROCESS-DELETION
    ELSE IF TRANSACTION-TYPE = "P"
        PERFORM PROCESS-PAYMENT
    ELSE IF TRANSACTION-TYPE = "C"
        PERFORM PROCESS-PHONE-CALL.



PROCESS-INSERTION.
    IF STATUS-OF-CURRENT-KEY = ALLOCATED
        MOVE ACCOUNTS-TRANSACTION-RECORD TO UPDATE-LOG-TRANSACTION
        WRITE UPDATE-LOG-RECORD
            FROM UPDATE-LOG-TRANSACTION-LINE AFTER 3
        MOVE "PHONE NO ALREADY ALLOCATED" TO UPDATE-LOG-MESSAGE
        WRITE UPDATE-LOG-RECORD
            FROM UPDATE-LOG-ERROR-LINE AFTER 1
    ELSE
        MOVE ALLOCATED TO STATUS-OF-CURRENT-KEY
        PERFORM CREATE-BILLING-ACTIVITY-RECORD
        MOVE TRANSACTION-PHONE-NUMBER TO
            MASTER-CUSTOMER-PHONE-NUMBER
        MOVE INSERTION-NAME TO MASTER-CUSTOMER-NAME
        MOVE INSERTION-ADDRESS TO MASTER-CUSTOMER-ADDRESS
        MOVE INSERTION-MONTHLY-CHARGE TO
            MASTER-BASIC-MONTHLY-CHARGE
        MOVE ZERO TO MASTER-ACCOUNT-BALANCE.



PROCESS-DELETION.
    IF STATUS-OF-CURRENT-KEY = UNALLOCATED
        MOVE ACCOUNTS-TRANSACTION-RECORD TO UPDATE-LOG-TRANSACTION
        WRITE UPDATE-LOG-RECORD
            FROM UPDATE-LOG-TRANSACTION-LINE AFTER 3
        MOVE "PHONE NO NOT ALLOCATED" TO UPDATE-LOG-MESSAGE
        WRITE UPDATE-LOG-RECORD
            FROM UPDATE-LOG-ERROR-LINE AFTER 1
    ELSE
        PERFORM CALCULATE-FINAL-BALANCE
        MOVE BILLING-CLOSING-BALANCE TO MASTER-ACCOUNT-BALANCE
        PERFORM SEND-SUMMARY-TO-CLOSED-FILE
        PERFORM SEND-ACCOUNT-TO-BILLING-FILE
        MOVE UNALLOCATED TO STATUS-OF-CURRENT-KEY.
```

```
PROCESS-PAYMENT.
    IF STATUS-OF-CURRENT-KEY = UNALLOCATED
        MOVE ACCOUNTS-TRANSACTION-RECORD TO UPDATE-LOG-TRANSACTION
        WRITE UPDATE-LOG-RECORD
            FROM UPDATE-LOG-TRANSACTION-LINE AFTER 3
        MOVE "PHONE NO NOT ALLOCATED" TO UPDATE-LOG-MESSAGE
        WRITE UPDATE-LOG-RECORD
            FROM UPDATE-LOG-ERROR-LINE AFTER 1
    ELSE
        ADD PAYMENT-AMOUNT TO BILLING-PAYMENTS-MADE.


PROCESS-PHONE-CALL.
    IF STATUS-OF-CURRENT-KEY = UNALLOCATED
        MOVE ACCOUNTS-TRANSACTION-RECORD TO UPDATE-LOG-TRANSACTION
        WRITE UPDATE-LOG-RECORD
            FROM UPDATE-LOG-TRANSACTION-LINE AFTER 3
        MOVE "PHONE NO NOT ALLOCATED" TO UPDATE-LOG-MESSAGE
        WRITE UPDATE-LOG-RECORD
            FROM UPDATE-LOG-ERROR-LINE AFTER 1
    ELSE
        ADD PHONE-CALL-COST TO BILLING-COST-OF-CALLS-MADE.


************************************************************
*                   BILLING ROUTINES                      *
************************************************************

CREATE-BILLING-ACTIVITY-RECORD.
    MOVE 0 TO BILLING-COST-OF-CALLS-MADE.
    MOVE 0 TO BILLING-PAYMENTS-MADE.


CALCULATE-FINAL-BALANCE.
    MOVE MASTER-ACCOUNT-BALANCE TO BILLING-OPENING-BALANCE.
    MOVE MASTER-BASIC-MONTHLY-CHARGE TO BILLING-MONTHLY-CHARGE.
    COMPUTE BILLING-TAX-ADDED  ROUNDED =
        ( BILLING-COST-OF-CALLS-MADE + BILLING-MONTHLY-CHARGE )
            * (TAX-RATE / 100.00).
    COMPUTE BILLING-CLOSING-BALANCE  ROUNDED =
        BILLING-OPENING-BALANCE +
        BILLING-COST-OF-CALLS-MADE +
        BILLING-MONTHLY-CHARGE +
        BILLING-TAX-ADDED -
        BILLING-PAYMENTS-MADE.


SEND-ACCOUNT-TO-BILLING-FILE.
    IF BILLING-CLOSING-BALANCE IS NOT ZERO
        MOVE MASTER-CUSTOMER-PHONE-NUMBER TO BILLING-PHONE-NUMBER
        MOVE MASTER-CUSTOMER-NAME TO BILLING-CUSTOMER-NAME
        MOVE MASTER-CUSTOMER-ADDRESS TO BILLING-CUSTOMER-ADDRESS
        WRITE BILLING-RECORD.
```

```
*********************************************************************
*                CLOSED ACCOUNT FILE ROUTINE(S)                    *
*********************************************************************

SEND-SUMMARY-TO-CLOSED-FILE.
    MOVE MASTER-CUSTOMER-PHONE-NUMBER TO CLOSED-PHONE-NUMBER.
    MOVE MASTER-CUSTOMER-NAME TO CLOSED-CUSTOMER-NAME.
    MOVE MASTER-CUSTOMER-ADDRESS TO CLOSED-CUSTOMER-ADDRESS.
    MOVE DELETION-DATE TO CLOSED-DATE.
    MOVE BILLING-CLOSING-BALANCE TO CLOSED-FINAL-BALANCE.
    WRITE CLOSED-ACCOUNT-RECORD.



*********************************************************************
*                     END OF PROGRAM                               *
*********************************************************************
```

9.5 SUMMARY

This chapter is primarily concerned with showing the COBOL coding of three typical data processing programs designed earlier in this book—a report program, a validate program, and a sequential file update program. All three programs stem directly from the designs expressed in pseudocode. In fact the correspondence is so close that the pseudocode design is clearly evident in the high level portions of the coding. Thus the need for documentation additional to the program text is reduced. Indeed, arguably, the pseudocode can be discarded, since it is duplicated in the code. If this superfluous documentation is thrown away the task of subsequent maintenance is eased, since only a single document has to be updated.

Coding standards such as are used by any experienced programmer have been suggested in this chapter. The program texts are illustrations of their application.

9.6 EXERCISES

1. Amend the report program from the Nu-wave Cosmetic Company given in this chapter to include the specification changes outlined in exercise 1 of Ch.3.

2. Extend the file update program for the telephone company as specified below:

    (a) Complete the implementation of the program components dealing with the creation and processing of the monthly activity records so that full details of all phone calls made by a customer are recorded in the billing file. See exercise 6.4.

(b) Section 6.8 of the text describes a problem which arises when an insertion transaction on a particular master file key is rejected as invalid and this transaction is followed by others on the same key. Amend the update program to ensure that ambiguous transactions are not applied during the update. Implement the solution described in section 6.8.

(c) Amend the program to improve the presentation of the update log report. Include at least page headings, page numbering and check totals of the total transactions seen, applied and rejected. Ensure that all routines dealing with the update log report are isolated in a separate module.

3. The code of the validate program contains a GO TO...DEPENDING ON statement in order to implement the **case** statement in the design. Recode this construction using the alternative of "chained" IF statements. Which implementation is easier to read in order to check the correctness? Which is easier to change, say, in the event of additional transaction codes?

4. Amend the validate program so as to improve the readability of the error report. Is this a straightforward task?

10

Top-down Implementation and Testing

10.1 INTRODUCTION

Previous chapters have dealt with program design and with coding. These two activities are sometimes collectively known as "implementation". In this chapter we discuss the subject of testing and the question of the *order* in which the design, coding and testing of the pieces of a large program should be done. We describe an approach to implementation and testing that is completely compatible with, and in accord with, functional decomposition. It is called top-down implementation and testing. In the next chapter we present an example of the use of the technique.

Top-down implementation and testing can be used in developing either a complete system of several dependent programs or just a single program.

10.2 TRADITIONAL METHODS

In referring to "traditional methods" no criticism is implied. It is, today, far from clear how to go about building systems and the arguments are far from over. We use this term to refer to the techniques that were in use in most programming shops before the advent of the new methods associated with the term "structured".

The traditional method of developing a system begins by breaking it down somehow into its constituent programs, subprograms and files. (The

170

methodologies for achieving this decomposition have been far from clear.)
Having drawn up detailed specifications of all the components, the project
proceeds by implementing the lowest level pieces of program, i.e. the ones
on which everything else depends. An immediate problem arises: "How can
we test these modules?" The usual technique, known as module or unit
testing, is to construct a "test harness" or "test bed" for each component.
This is another program whose sole function is to invoke the component
under test in a way that is consistent with its eventual role in the complete
system. Probably test data is also required. A diagram of low level components and their test harnesses is shown in Fig. 10.1. One matter of immediate

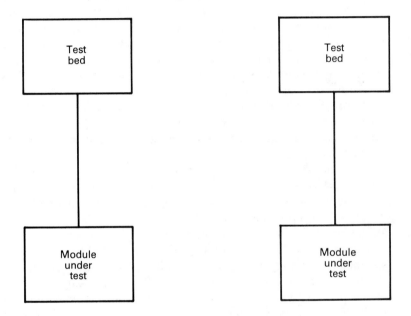

Fig. 10.1 Bottom-up testing.

note is that a test harness may be a complex program, requiring considerable
development and testing time itself. Preparation of the test data may also
involve considerable effort.

When the lowest level components have been tested in this way, modules are combined into subsystems that are tested in a similar manner, again
using a test harness. The procedure continues until the complete system is
finally assembled and tested as a whole.

This, then, is the traditional bottom-up method of testing. It suffers
from the following drawbacks:

(a)   Much time can be spent on the construction of test harnesses and test data. Worse still, they are sometimes thrown away when testing is complete. This has been likened to the act of a carpenter, who, having made him or herself a new set of tools specially to build a new house, destroys the tools when the house is complete. (The analogy is intended to demonstrate the waste of effort that is involved.) Alternatively, test beds and test data are retained so that when enhancements or corrections are carried out it can be ensured that the components that worked previously still work. In this case the test material has itself to be stored and maintained, consuming more valuable effort.

(b)   Errors that are found at the integration stages of subsystem testing require repetition of the whole process of designing, coding and unit testing. Subsystems or components may have to be repeatedly reworked as more and more of the system is integrated. It is common experience that system testing accounts for the major proportion (roughly between a third and a half) of a project timescale.

(c)   Because testing of the complete system is carried out towards the end of the project, it is often the case that major flaws in the system design are not discovered until near the planned completion time. The discovery leads often to the reconstruction of large parts of the system at a very embarassing time.

(d)   There is no visible, working system until the very last stage, system testing, is complete. True, there are tested components and subsystems, but there is normally nothing that can be demonstrated to the client as even providing a limited capability.

(e)   With bottom-up testing the use of computer facilities is most concentrated during the last stage of the project, integrated testing. Time is spent almost entirely in repeatedly running tests of significant parts of the system and in carrying out recompilation and linking.

(f)   Heavy pressure on the available computer facilities can compound the problems of a team already struggling to meet a deadline. No wonder that long hours of work result and, in turn, mistakes occur as circumstances appear to conspire against the project.

Top-down development helps to avoid some of these problems, as we explain later.

10.3   TESTING

Every programmer knows the tedium of devising test data for his or her programs. The guidelines for testing have become part of the folklore of programming:

(a)   Construct test data that ensures that every possible path within the program is executed at least once. (This does not mean every possible combination of paths: that would be an impossibly large task.)

(b)   Use extreme values of the test data. The idea is presumably to push the program to its limits.

(c)   Before running a test, write down the expected outcome. This avoids our natural tendency to modify our expectations to comply with the actual outcome.

There is an alternative school of thought on testing which says that test data should be invented solely on the basis of the program specification and in particular in ignorance of the program structure. Preferably someone other than the programmer should draw up the test data so that there is no unconscious influence on the choice of data. Although this approach has all the appeal of independent auditing, it does suffer from the criticism that many program statements can go untested.

Perhaps the most important comment on testing was made by E. W. Dijkstra: "testing can only show the presence of bugs, never their absence". In other words, no matter how conscientiously we test our programs, we can never be sure that they are bug free. This causes us to recall Murphy's law: "If a system can fail it will", and its addendum: "and at the worst possible moment."

These sayings sound glib, but unfortunately they have an undercurrent of truth. They suggest to us that we should recognize the limitations of testing and perhaps concentrate more on other methods of trying to make programs reliable—methods that try to ensure that bugs are avoided or eliminated during the *design* of a program. Nonetheless, at the present state of the art there seems to be no effective substitute for thorough testing. The only contribution of the new "structured" methods to testing is the technique of top-down development, described next.

10.4   TOP-DOWN DEVELOPMENT

Top-down development is an alternative approach to traditional methods that proceeds as follows. Design commences as usual with the highest-level components of the system or program. However, before lower levels are designed, the highest level is coded. In a batch system this highest level is probably the job control language statements (these may be as complex as the programs themselves); in an on-line system it may be a controlling program. Program "stubs" are used to stand in for invoked but as yet unwritten lower level components. These stubs are rudimentary replacements for missing COBOL programs, paragraphs or subprograms.

A stub may carry out:

(a) an easily written simulation of the final action of the component
or
(b) the output of a message indicating that the component has been
     executed.

Test data is constructed as necessary and the system is assembled and
tested. An immediate outcome is that we can very quickly have something
that works. Moreover, it is the most crucial part of the system. We also can
have something that can be demonstrated to the client as performing some
imitation of the total system.

Implementation proceeds by selecting lower level components (formerly stubs) one at a time for design and coding and incorporation into the
system. In general, at any stage in the development there are:

(a) higher level components which have already been tested
(b) a single component under test
(c) stubs.

Figure 10.2 illustrates this scheme.

Clearly, development will not, and should not, always proceed according to the above textbook prescription. Some variations of the method and
some difficulties that may arise are as follows:

First, development will not always proceed on a rigid level-by-level
basis. In practice some low-level components need to be designed, coded
and tested at an early stage. An example might be the development of those
parts of a program or system that produce a report. The report could be
shown to the eventual user of the program who might, as usual, request
modifications. The sooner these are sorted out the better.

Second, some programmers favor a variation of the approach we have
described. They fear that having translated some of their design into code
and tested it, they will later find that, as a result of developing lower level
components, there is a mistake in the higher level components. This would
necessitate annoying redesign, recoding and retesting. An alternative
approach, which retains many of the benefits of the method, is to complete
the design of the entire program or system before embarking on top-down
coding and testing.

Finally, another objection to strict use of the method is that it is often
much easier in terms of both the programmer's time and computer time to
test a component in isolation rather than as a part of the higher level system.
Indeed sometimes it is difficult in top-down testing to generate adequate test
data for a module. In cases where this is true, it may be best that the new
component is incorporated in good time to test its interfaces in its true
environment.

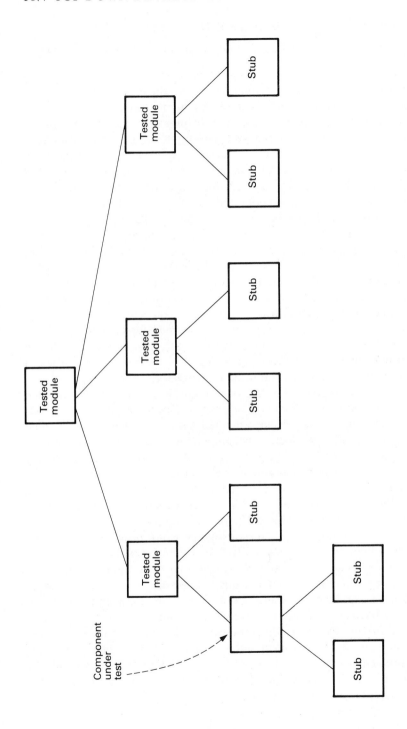

Fig. 10.2 Top-down testing.

10.5   AN ASSESSMENT OF THE METHOD

Some of the claims made for top-down implementation are as follows:

(a)   *Early detection of major flaws.* One of the main problems with bottom-up development is that faults with the highest level of design are not discovered until the complete system is tested—at the very end of the project. Such major design problems can require the reconstruction of large parts of the system. On the other hand, top-down development ensures that the major components and interfaces are tested first, when any errors can be corrected without rewriting a lot of program. Thus the method can reduce the effort spent in developing a system and help with meeting the completion deadline.

     The argument assumes that the higher-level parts of a program are in some sense the most important. On the contrary, however, it may well be that some low-level aspect of the problem, in the data perhaps, has been neglected and is crucial. If top-down development is being employed this could lead to major redesign effort at a late stage.

(b)   *Reliability.* Once incorporated into top-down testing, software components are thereafter tested again and again, acting as test beds for lower level parts of the program. With so much repeated testing of the final code (rather than temporary test beds), there is a greater chance of detecting faults. Note also that it will be the higher level program components that will tend to be most reliable.

(c)   *Program debugging.* Finding out exactly where a fault is located is easier in top-down implementation. This is because stubs are replaced one at a time by the fully implemented component. Thus any fault must be localized in the single new component or in its interface with the higher level modules. In contrast, in a bottom-up environment, usually a number of components are combined together for the first time in a single step. So in this case any errors which arise are due to faults in any of the new components or any of the newly tried interfaces. This poses a much more formidable problem of pinpointing.

     Note, however, that this advantage is not peculiar to top-down implementation—it is shared by any scheme in which just one new component is incorporated at a time. (This is sometimes known as "incremental testing".) What top-down testing does is to systematically create situations where incremental testing is straightforward: but the same *can* be done in a bottom-up fashion.

(d)   *Use of computer time.* In top-down implementation the use of the computer system for compilation, linking and particularly testing is spread much more evenly throughout project lifetime. This avoids the extreme pressure that tends to be encountered towards the end of the project in the bottom-up approach.

(e) *Morale.* A feature of top-down implementation can be the appearance of a tangible, working system at a very early stage in the development of the software. Although the system does not have the full capabilities of the final system, its presence can reassure managers, clients and the members of a team that something has actually been produced and that the full system is not too far away.

(f) *Programmers' time.* Overall top-down implementation may involve significantly less programmers' time. Two reasons have already been mentioned—the early detection of major flaws (reducing rework), and the fast location of bugs. But perhaps the greatest saving is in constructing test beds and test data. In top-down implementation and testing, test beds do not need to be constructed, as the already-tested higher level part of the program acts in this role. Although program stubs do need to be constructed, they tend to be significantly simpler. Similarly the data that is prepared to test the whole system can often be used from the start in the top-down method, avoiding the time spent in devising data especially for each unit test.

Top-down development is a technique that is said to be well-suited to projects that are undertaken by a team of programmers. Some of the difficulties of working in teams are discussed later in this book, but there is one issue that relates particularly to this method. Top-down development begins with the complete implementation of the highest levels of the program or system. In most organizations this would be carried out by a single Senior Programmer. At this stage, therefore, there is nothing for the other, possibly more junior, members of the team to do. There can be a strong temptation to assign to the other members of the team the development of some low-level modules that are expected to be required. This is a tendency that should be resisted, since it brings with it all the problems inherent in bottom-up development. One solution to this problem is to delay the assignment of programmers to the project until the high-level parts of the system are complete. It requires careful planning, but no more so than any other development scheme.

10.6 SUMMARY

In this chapter we have described the traditional bottom-up approach to implementation and testing and identified some of its weaknesses. We have described the technique of top-down implementation and explained its apparent advantages and disadvantages in comparison with the bottom-up approach. Evidence from practical experience of using top-down implementation confirms that the major benefits are:

(a) less programmer time is spent on debugging and testing
(b) less computer time is consumed
(c) there is better awareness of the progress of the project
(d) the software that is produced is more reliable.

Finally we should remind ourselves of the limitations of any kind of testing as a technique for pursuing the goal of software reliability.

In the next chapter we present a practical illustration of the use of top-down implementation.

11

Implementation of an On-line Update

11.1 INTRODUCTION

In this chapter we present a worked example of the construction of a piece of software using the technique of top-down implementation and testing described in the last chapter. We develop a program that is large enough to demonstrate the principles of the techniques, but so as to avoid unnecessary length the problem is not sufficiently complex to be fully realistic.

The application is an on-line update, a type which is becoming increasingly common. The program is required to accept a request from a terminal operator, access a file of information and then reply to the terminal. This is to be done repetitively: response within a short time is required. Clearly it is unlikely that the requirement for fast access will be satisfied by a sequential file.

11.2 THE SPECIFICATION

The task is to construct a program to implement a rudimentary airline seat reservation system. The program should accept various commands keyed in at interactive terminals and act upon them. Each command begins with one of the words:

create   to add a new flight to the system
delete   to remove a flight from the system
reserve to make a passenger reservation
cancel   to cancel a reservation
list   to request a passenger list

Each command occupies a single line. A command word is followed by parameters. The command word and parameters are separated by one or more spaces. The details of the commands, their functions, and parameters, are given below. A ⟨number⟩ consists of exactly three digits, and a ⟨name⟩ contains up to 20 alphanumeric characters and periods. Each command produces some output, either an error message indicating an illegal argument or request, or a confirmation of the successful completion of the command.

> **create** ⟨number⟩
> The flight numbered ⟨number⟩ is added to the system. The attempted addition of a duplicate flight is an error.
> **delete** ⟨number⟩
> The flight numbered ⟨number⟩ is deleted from the system. The removal of a non-existent flight is an error.
> **reserve** ⟨number⟩ ⟨name⟩
> Add a passenger to the flight numbered ⟨number⟩. Passengers' names need not be unique. It is an error to seat a passenger on a flight that does not exist.
> **cancel** ⟨number⟩ ⟨name⟩
> Remove the passenger with the name ⟨name⟩ from the flight with number ⟨number⟩. It is an error to remove a passenger from a flight that does not exist or to remove a passenger from a flight on which he or she is not booked.
> **list** ⟨number⟩
> Print an alphabetical list of the names of the passengers on the flight numbered ⟨number⟩. It is an error if the flight does not exist.

Assume that the main store of the computer is inadequate to hold all the required information, so that use of a file is necessary.

11.3   FIRST THOUGHTS

We see that the programmer has implicitly been given responsibility for designing the file and perhaps this is rather unusual. This is not a book on file design and we do not wish to dwell on the subject. Almost certainly a sequential file will be inadequate, but the choice of indexed sequential or direct access file structure will be determined by factors which have not been specified—for example, the mechanism by which flight numbers are allocated and the length of time that the system must maintain information on flights.

As we study the program structure using top-down decomposition we see that the program can be seen as two major components:

(a)   a part that interacts with the human user of the program, accepting commands, analyzing and checking them and displaying messages

(b)   a part that accesses the file.

This structure is shown in a diagram in Fig. 11.1.

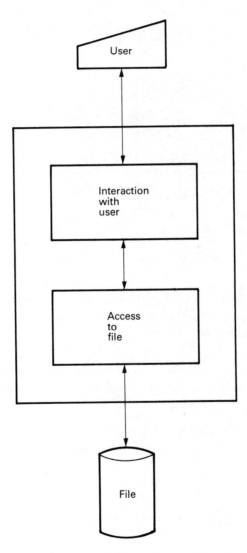

Fig. 11.1   Structure of the on-line update program.

As we carry out the process of top-down implementation and testing it becomes natural to complete that part of the program that interacts with the user, leaving the remainder as stubs. Thorough testing can take place at this stage with no need for a file of flight information. Indeed, at this stage the file need not even be designed! This illustrates the principle of data hiding—all aspects of file structure, access and update are embodied in a single software component whose workings are invisible from the outside.

Regrettably COBOL provides no good way of representing this situation clearly. It is not possible to construct a subprogram which has the several necessary entry points and which hides all information about the file structure and access methods.

11.4 THE PROGRAM DESIGN

The essential part of the algorithm must be a loop which, repeated indefinitely, accepts commands and processes them:

> *initialize*
> **perform** *read and process command*
>   **until** forever

But for the purpose of testing it is probably more convenient to set up test data in a file rather than to exercise the program interactively. So if the program is to process an input file it is perhaps clearer to make the loop terminate like this:

> *initialize*
> **perform** *read and process command*
>   **until** command = finish
> *terminate processing*
> stop

(Testing in this manner will help to establish the correctness of the program, but it doesn't give information on whether the program is meeting its requirements for response time.)

The decomposition of the most significant component is:

> *read and process command*
>   *prepare for input*
>   read command
>   *scan the line*
>   **if** no errors

then
  act on command
else
  display error message
else

The breakdown of the other two components from the top level are:

initialize
  open file to access terminal
  initialize file of flight information
  display system startup message

terminate processing
  display system closedown message
  terminate file of flight information
  close file to access terminal

We note that as we have decided to delay considering those parts of the program that access the file of flight information, the statements:

initialize file of flight information

and

terminate file of flight information

will be implemented as program stubs.
  Continuing the design of the program we next develop:

scan the line
  analyze command
  if no error
  then *skip spaces*
  endif
  if no error
  then *analyze number*
  endif

We have now expressed the algorithm in terms of three program components that together inspect the string of characters that have been input, and one component that actually carries out a request. We have also made the decision that if the command word that is entered is erroneous, then no attempt is made to analyze the remainder of the input. If there are no errors then a command is acted upon as follows:

> *act on command*
>   **case** command **of**
>   reserve: *process reserve seat*
>   create : *process create flight*
>   delete : *process delete flight*
>   cancel : *process cancel seat*
>   list   : *process list flight*
>   **endcase**

Turning to the scanning of input lines, we observe that as the commands are in free format they must be examined a character at a time. So we indulge in a little bottom-up design for a component that will supply characters one at a time from the input record. We try to design a piece of program that will be generally useful, rather than thinking about its role in a specific context. When performed, the paragraph will provide the next character in the line, except that when the end of the line is reached, a special "end of line" character will be provided.

The alternative to creating this module is to have references to the input line and its subscript, and tests for the end of the line scattered throughout the program. It is arguably clearer to concentrate all this in one place. The algorithm is:

> *get next character*
>   **if** character number > line length
>   **then** character is end of line
>   **else**
>   character is line (character number)
>   add 1 to character number
>   **endif**

There is nothing particularly interesting in the algorithms for:

> *analyze command,*
> *skip spaces*

and

> *analyze number*

and so we do not give them here. (Their COBOL equivalents are shown later.)

The decomposition has proceeded to a level of detail where there is a significant amount of logic that can be tested. Besides, if the lower level components are developed much more, some knowledge of the file structure will be necessary, and this is a complication we wish to postpone until we are convinced of the reliability of the current system. So we stop the design at this stage, and elect to implement undeveloped components as stubs.

11.5 THE COBOL CODE AND THE TESTING

The COBOL text for that part of the program so far designed is shown below. It corresponds closely to the pseudocode. The program stubs are at the end. Their function is either to cause a message to be displayed or else to do nothing.

```
DATA DIVISION.

FILE SECTION.

FD   PRINT-FILE              LABEL RECORDS OMITTED.

01   PRINT-LINE.
     02   FILLER             PIC X(9).
     02   MESSAGE-X          PIC X(30).
     02   FILLER             PIC X(33).

FD   INPUT-FILE              LABEL RECORDS OMITTED.

01   INPUT-LINE.
     02   INPUT-CHARACTER    PIC X          OCCURS 80.

WORKING-STORAGE SECTION.

01   ERROR-CONTROL.
     02   ERROR-STATE        PIC 9.
     02   YES                PIC 9          VALUE IS 1.
     02   NONE               PIC 9          VALUE IS 0.

01   SCANNING-THE-LINE.
     02   CHAR-NUM           PIC 99.
     02   LINE-LENGTH        PIC 99         VALUE IS 80.
     02   CHAR               PIC X.
     02   END-OF-LINE        PIC X          VALUE IS "*".

01   ANALYZING-COMMAND-WORDS.
     02   INPUT-COMMAND         PIC X(8).
          88   RESERVE-MESSAGE        VALUE "RESERVE ".
          88   CREATE-MESSAGE         VALUE "CREATE  ".
          88   DELETE-MESSAGE         VALUE "DELETE  ".
          88   CANCEL-MESSAGE         VALUE "CANCEL  ".
          88   LIST-MESSAGE           VALUE "LIST    ".
          88   SYSTEM-TERMINATE       VALUE "FINISH  ".

     02   INPUT-COMMAND-X REDEFINES INPUT-COMMAND.
          03   COMMAND-CHARACTER   PIC X     OCCURS 8.

     02      LETTER-NUM         PIC 9.

01   ANALYZING-FLIGHT-NUMBER.
     02   FLIGHT-NUMBER.
          03   FLIGHT-CHAR     PIC X         OCCURS 3.
     02   DIGIT-NUM            PIC 9.
```

```
01  MESSAGES.
    02  RESERVE-ENTERED      PIC X(30)
        VALUE IS "RESERVE STUB ENTERED          ".
    02  CREATE-ENTERED       PIC X(30)
        VALUE IS "CREATE STUB ENTERED           ".
    02  DELETE-ENTERED       PIC X(30)
        VALUE IS "DELETE STUB ENTERED           ".
    02  CANCEL-ENTERED       PIC X(30)
        VALUE IS "CANCEL STUB ENTERED           ".
    02  LIST-ENTERED         PIC X(30)
        VALUE IS "LIST STUB ENTERED             ".
    02  OPENING-MESSAGE      PIC X(30)
        VALUE IS "SYSTEM NOW READY              ".
    02  CLOSE-MESSAGE        PIC X(30)
        VALUE IS "SYSTEM NOW GOING OFF LINE     ".
    02  REPEAT-MESSAGE       PIC X(30)
        VALUE IS "COMMAND IGNORED               ".
    02  ENTER-MESSAGE        PIC X(30)
        VALUE IS "PLEASE ENTER COMMAND          ".
    02  INVALID-MESSAGE      PIC X(30)
        VALUE IS "INVALID COMMAND               ".
    02  INVALID-FLIGHT-MESS PIC X(30)
        VALUE IS "INVALID FLIGHT NUMBER FORMAT  ".
    02  PROCESSED-MESSAGE    PIC X(30)
        VALUE IS "COMMAND PROCESSED             ".



***************************************************************
*   HIGH LEVEL LOGIC                                          *
***************************************************************

PROCEDURE DIVISION.

MAIN.
    PERFORM INITIALIZE.
    PERFORM READ-AND-PROCESS-A-COMMAND
            UNTIL  SYSTEM-TERMINATE.
    PERFORM END-ROUTINE.
    STOP RUN.



***************************************************************
*   INITIALIZATION AND TERMINATION                           *
***************************************************************

INITIALIZE.
    OPEN INPUT   INPUT-FILE
         OUTPUT PRINT-FILE.
    PERFORM INITIALIZE-FILE.
    MOVE SPACES TO PRINT-LINE.
    MOVE OPENING-MESSAGE TO MESSAGE-X.
    PERFORM PRINT-AFTER-2.
```

```
END-ROUTINE.
     MOVE CLOSE-MESSAGE TO MESSAGE-X.
     PERFORM PRINT-AFTER-2.
     PERFORM TERMINATE-FILE.
     CLOSE INPUT-FILE
          PRINT-FILE.


**********************************************************************
*    ANALYSIS OF A LINE OF INPUT                                    *
**********************************************************************


  READ-AND-PROCESS-A-COMMAND.
     PERFORM PREPARE-FOR-INPUT.
     PERFORM READ-COMMAND.
     PERFORM SCAN-THE-LINE.
     IF ERROR-STATE = NONE
          PERFORM ACT-ON-COMMAND
          MOVE PROCESSED-MESSAGE TO MESSAGE-X
          PERFORM PRINT-AFTER-1
     ELSE
          IF NOT SYSTEM-TERMINATE
             MOVE REPEAT-MESSAGE TO MESSAGE-X
             PERFORM PRINT-AFTER-2.

  PREPARE-FOR-INPUT.
     MOVE ENTER-MESSAGE TO MESSAGE-X.
     PERFORM PRINT-AFTER-2.
     MOVE NONE TO ERROR-STATE.
     MOVE 1 TO CHAR-NUM.
     MOVE "*" TO CHAR.

  SCAN-THE-LINE.
     PERFORM ANALYZE-COMMAND.
     IF ERROR-STATE = NONE
          PERFORM SKIP-SPACES.
     IF ERROR-STATE = NONE
          PERFORM ANALYZE-NUMBER.

  READ-COMMAND.
     READ INPUT-FILE AT END MOVE "FINISH  " TO INPUT-LINE.
     MOVE INPUT-LINE TO PRINT-LINE.
     PERFORM PRINT-AFTER-2.

**********************************************************************
*  LOW LEVEL ROUTINES CONCERNED WITH SCANNING TEXT                  *
**********************************************************************


  GET-NEXT-CHARACTER.
     IF CHAR-NUM IS GREATER THAN LINE-LENGTH
          MOVE END-OF-LINE TO CHAR
     ELSE
          MOVE INPUT-CHARACTER (CHAR-NUM) TO CHAR
          ADD 1 TO CHAR-NUM.
```

```
SKIP-SPACES.
    PERFORM GET-NEXT-CHARACTER
        UNTIL CHAR NOT = SPACE.


****************************************************************
*    ANALYSIS OF A COMMAND WORD                               *
****************************************************************


ANALYZE-COMMAND.
    PERFORM MOVE-COMMAND.
    IF NOT (RESERVE-MESSAGE OR
            CREATE-MESSAGE   OR
            DELETE-MESSAGE   OR
            CANCEL-MESSAGE   OR
            LIST-MESSAGE     OR
            SYSTEM-TERMINATE)
        MOVE INVALID-MESSAGE TO MESSAGE-X
        PERFORM PRINT-AFTER-2
        MOVE YES TO ERROR-STATE.
    IF  SYSTEM-TERMINATE
        MOVE YES TO ERROR-STATE.



MOVE-COMMAND.
    MOVE 1 TO LETTER-NUM.
    MOVE SPACES TO INPUT-COMMAND.
    PERFORM MOVE-LETTER
        UNTIL
            CHAR = SPACE
            OR
            LETTER-NUM = 9.



MOVE-LETTER.
    PERFORM GET-NEXT-CHARACTER.
    MOVE CHAR TO COMMAND-CHARACTER (LETTER-NUM).
    ADD 1 TO LETTER-NUM.

****************************************************************
*    ANALYSIS OF THE FLIGHT NUMBER                            *
****************************************************************


ANALYZE-NUMBER.
    PERFORM MOVE-NUMBER.
    IF ERROR-STATE = YES
        MOVE INVALID-FLIGHT-MESS TO MESSAGE-X
        PERFORM PRINT-AFTER-1.
```

```
MOVE-NUMBER.
      PERFORM MOVE-DIGIT VARYING DIGIT-NUM
            FROM 1 BY 1 UNTIL DIGIT-NUM = 4.
      IF FLIGHT-NUMBER IS NOT NUMERIC
         MOVE YES TO ERROR-STATE.
      IF NOT (CHAR = SPACE OR CHAR = END-OF-LINE)
         MOVE YES TO ERROR-STATE.



MOVE-DIGIT.
      MOVE CHAR TO FLIGHT-CHAR (DIGIT-NUM).
      PERFORM GET-NEXT-CHARACTER.



PRINT-AFTER-1.
      WRITE PRINT-LINE AFTER 1.
      MOVE SPACES TO PRINT-LINE.



PRINT-AFTER-2.
      WRITE PRINT-LINE AFTER 2.
      MOVE SPACES TO PRINT-LINE.

**********************************************************************
*  SWITCH ON COMMAND WORD                                            *
**********************************************************************

ACT-ON-COMMAND.
      IF RESERVE-MESSAGE
         PERFORM RESERVE-SEAT
      ELSE IF CREATE-MESSAGE
              PERFORM CREATE-FLIGHT
      ELSE IF DELETE-MESSAGE
              PERFORM DELETE-FLIGHT
      ELSE IF CANCEL-MESSAGE
              PERFORM CANCEL-SEAT
      ELSE IF LIST-MESSAGE
              PERFORM LIST-FLIGHT.



**********************************************************************
*  PROGRAM STUBS                                                     *
**********************************************************************

RESERVE-SEAT.
      MOVE RESERVE-ENTERED TO MESSAGE-X.
      PERFORM PRINT-AFTER-2.
```

```
CREATE-FLIGHT.
     MOVE CREATE-ENTERED TO MESSAGE-X.
     PERFORM PRINT-AFTER-2.


DELETE-FLIGHT.
     MOVE DELETE-ENTERED TO MESSAGE-X.
     PERFORM PRINT-AFTER-2.


CANCEL-SEAT.
     MOVE CANCEL-ENTERED TO MESSAGE-X.
     PERFORM PRINT-AFTER-2.


LIST-FLIGHT.
     MOVE LIST-ENTERED TO MESSAGE-X.
     PERFORM PRINT-AFTER-2.


INITIALIZE-FILE.


TERMINATE-FILE.


*********************************************************************
*              END OF PROGRAM                                      *
*********************************************************************
```

This program can and has been thoroughly tested in its incomplete form. Some typical output from it is as follows:

```
SYSTEM NOW READY

        PLEASE ENTER COMMAND
LIST    123

        LIST STUB ENTERED
        COMMAND PROCESSED

        PLEASE ENTER COMMAND
```

```
CREATE   1234

         INVALID FLIGHT NUMBER FORMAT

         COMMAND IGNORED

         PLEASE ENTER COMMAND

RESERVE

         INVALID FLIGHT NUMBER FORMAT

         COMMAND IGNORED

         PLEASE ENTER COMMAND

HELLO

         INVALID COMMAND

         COMMAND IGNORED

         PLEASE ENTER COMMAND
```

We do not show the remainder of the development of this program. The next step is to design the file structure and access method, and then design and code the program components that have until now been implemented as stubs. Each stub is replaced in turn by its full COBOL version and the system tested. There can be considerable confidence that any error is due to a fault in a newly incorporated component.

11.6 SUMMARY

We have illustrated the process of top-down implementation and testing by means of an example. We have also demonstrated the technique of designing a low-level program component in a bottom-up manner. Applying our design method in this example leads to a structure in two major parts—one to analyse and check text strings, and one to access a file. This second piece of program illustrates the principle of data hiding (described in Chapter 4) in which only a minimal set of components act upon and therefore know about a file structure.

11.7 EXERCISE

Continue and, if you have time, complete the development of the program using the technique of top-down implementation and testing. In order to continue the design some decision will have to be taken about the structure and accessing of the file or files involved. This will partly depend on what facilities are available to you on your computer.

Firstly design and implement "initialize file" and "terminate file", and then test the complete system. Then develop "create a flight" and test the complete system again. Continue in this way implementing components one by one and testing the whole system after the incorporation of a new part.

12

Structured
Walkthroughs

12.1 INTRODUCTION

A structured walkthrough is the faddish term for an organized meeting at which a program (or some other product) is examined. A major aim of the meeting is to try to find bugs which might otherwise go undetected for some time. (There are other goals, which are explained later.) The word "structured" simply means "well organized". The term "walkthrough" derives from the activity of a programmer explaining step by step the working of his or her program. Most programmers have had the experience of spending hours or even days puzzling over the incomprehensible behavior of a program, only to find that the bug is glaringly obvious once identified. It is also common to find that what you just cannot see is perfectly obvious to someone else. The reasoning behind structured walkthroughs is just this: that by letting other people look at your program, errors will be found much more quickly.

You might react by saying, "What's so new about that? I've always gone to others to seek advice when I have a problem. Structured walkthroughs are obviously just another fad which is really commonsense!" There is some truth in the criticism. However, we have all seen the situation where a program has been used in production for some time before a failure arises which is attributable to some simple programming error. The evidence suggests that structured walkthroughs can greatly reduce such problems, as well as saving programmers' time in other ways.

Consider the traditional way in which a programmer works. Given a clear specification, a programmer may well carry out the complete process of

193

program design, coding and testing entirely on his or her own. Only if he or she cannot understand some aspect of the computer system to be used or the specification that has been given will he or she seek clarification. In many organizations programmers are expected to be quiet backroom technicians in contrast to the articulate extrovert systems analysts. Any discussion or sharing of ideas that is not absolutely in the line of duty is frowned upon. In an open plan office where all activities are on view, a programmer can be made to feel that the only acceptable mode of behavior is to be seen sitting at the desk "working", that is either reading or writing, but not talking. A program is regarded as a work of art, that is the creation of an individual programmer. These attitudes tend to deny that "two heads are better than one", that through talking with others you can produce better work.

Credit for the invention of structured walkthroughs has been given to Weinberg, in his book, *The Psychology of Computer Programming*.[1] He suggests that programmers see their programs as an extension of themselves. They are unable to see errors in their own programs, since to do so would be to find a fault in themselves, and this, apparently, is unacceptable. Hence the need for others to help with fault finding.

This chapter describes the conduct of structured walkthroughs, which have to be well organized to be effective. It discusses some of the apprehensions that programmers may suffer, faced with the adoption of this technique. Finally, we suggest that if emotional difficulties are overcome, structured walkthroughs can make the programmer's life more interesting as well as contributing towards better programs.

12.2 ORGANIZATION

The Scope of Walkthroughs

Although the idea of structured walkthroughs has had its biggest impact in dealing with the examination of program code, the technique can be useful at many stages throughout the development of a computer-based system.

As regards the programming part of a project, walkthroughs can be concerned with reviewing:

(a)   the program specification
(b)   the program design (pseudocode)
(c)   the COBOL code
(d)   the test data
(e)   the results of testing
(f)   the program documention.

The walkthrough aims to identify the following sorts of problems in programs:

(a)   omissions, inconsistency or ambiguity in the specification
(b)   flaws in the program design
(c)   unclear logic in the program design or code
(d)   inefficient coding
(e)   adequacy of the test data
(f)   correctness of the test results
(g)   inadequate or unclear documentation.

But structured walkthroughs can and have been used to check work at various stages during a complete project. For example:

(a)   the system specification
(b)   the overall design of the software in terms of its constituent programs
(c)   the plans for the time scales of the project
(d)   the work assignments and schedules
(e)   the user guides.

Membership

Who should be present at a structured walkthrough? The more people there are, the greater the scope for time-wasting, due to differences of opinion. With fewer people, there may be less formality and contention, but fewer errors uncovered. There are snags and benefits, however many are involved.

At one extreme it can be very helpful for a programmer just to informally ask a colleague to look at his/her work. This is completely informal with no minutes or reporting. A more usual walkthrough involves from three to six people; any more tends to be too many. However many people there are, they should carry out the following roles (some may have to carry out more than one):

(a)   the programmer whose work is to be studied
(b)   a chairperson, whose job is to ensure that the meeting is conducted in an orderly way. He or she should, for example, try to curtail prolonged arguments
(c)   a secretary, who records decisions. This is not an onerous job because it is only the brief summary of the points that need to be kept
(d)   someone who is viewing the material from the point of view of perhaps having to maintain it in years to come
(e)   someone who is examining the program to see whether it conforms to the standards of the organization
(f)   a user, someone who is looking at the material from the point of view of the potential user of the software.

We must emphasize that these roles need not be carried out by appropriate specialists. In fact usually all the participants will be programmers, carrying out the different jobs.

Note that we are not suggesting that the project leader or any representative of management is present at the walkthrough. Such a presence is highly likely to stifle free and frank discussion and make the programmer presenting his or her work feel threatened. This can only damage the effectiveness of the walkthrough.

Before the Walkthrough

There is a lot to be done in careful preparation before a walkthrough takes place. Obviously the participants must be chosen, and informed of the date, time and venue of the meeting. But those attending must also be issued with copies of the material for review. It is vital that they study it carefully prior to the meeting, making notes as they do so. Clearly they require adequate time to do this. Choice of the right amount of material to review is critical. If there is too much material the participants will be disinclined to tackle it. More important, if there is a lot of material, then a lot of time will have been spent on it, and it may be riddled with errors. This means that the walkthrough itself will be a long and tortuous session and afterwards the programmer will have to spend a long time redoing a lot of his or her work. So it is most important that the material for review is carefully chosen. Experience has shown that the timing of a walkthrough is critical; walkthroughs which discover no errors are too early and walkthroughs which discover a multitude of errors are too late. It is suggested that the amount of work that should be reviewed at one meeting should be 50 to 100 lines of COBOL program or 1–3 pages of pseudocode or 5–10 pages of written specification. Given this sort of quantity of material, the participants should each spend up to about one hour in studying it.

During the Walkthrough

The purpose of the walkthrough meeting is to locate and record any problems with the material under review. In order to do this in a systematic manner the main thing that happens is that the programmer whose material is being reviewed explains his or her work step by step. The other participants intervene from time to time with criticisms or suggestions.

What are the reviewers looking for in examining material? It depends, of course, on the exact nature of the material, but may include:

(a) ambiguity or incompleteness in a specification
(b) a program that does not meet its specification
(c) a program design that does not achieve the effect that the programmer intended
(d) a program that would be difficult to change to meet new requirements
(e) a coding error
(f) incomplete or unclear documentation
(g) material that does not conform to the standards of the organization
(h) inadequacies in test data.

Any petty errors should not be allowed to slow down the meeting. For this reason, the reviewers should hand to the reviewee programmer at the start of the meeting lists of any minor typing, spelling, grammatical or syntax errors that they have found. These items will not be discussed in the meeting.

Once a problem is isolated the meeting should not attempt to solve it. This is too difficult and time consuming in a group situation. It is for the programmer to sort out the cause of the error, and rectify it, after the meeting. He or she may, of course, seek advice (after the meeting) from one of the participants. But the meeting itself is concerned only with identifying problems. Note also that problems are not *discovered* at the meeting; this should have been done previously, during preparation.

When participants at a meeting are pointing out errors it helps if they can do it in a diplomatic manner, so as not to embarass or intimidate the reviewer. Rather than criticize the programmer, remarks should be directed at the program as if it were an independent object. The critic should say, "I think there may be a problem in handling..." rather than, "Look what a stupid error you have made here." Such concern for others can only lead to a better working atmosphere and more effective structured walkthroughs.

As the meeting proceeds the secretary records the faults that are identified. Do not worry that these need to be detailed minutes, painstakingly comprehensive. A concise list of points is all that is necessary. For example, an entry might say "program ignores end of file".

Clearly the role of the chairperson is crucial. He or she tries to ensure that the meeting is effective. If this is not done, people in the organization will not have faith in walkthroughs. The chairperson should ensure that progress takes place in a logical, step-by-step order. If necessary he or she should insist that suggestions are postponed until the appropriate time within the meeting. The chairperson should try to curtail unnecessary discussion or digression by gently pointing out that this is happening and insisting that the meeting returns to the essential issues.

The chairperson should try to ensure that the meeting is short. This promotes a more business-like approach at the meeting and helps prevent fatigue and boredom setting in. We suggest that the aim should be for the walkthrough to take half an hour and that it should not be allowed to go on after an hour. This duration is consistent with reviewing the quantities of material suggested earlier.

One way in which the walkthrough may be kept under control is to start the meeting by getting everyone to agree on the rules of conduct, the time allowed and the power of the chairperson. More normally, though, these rules of conduct are standardized throughout an organization.

Although we have suggested that the central guiding activity of the meeting is the programmer explaining his or her work, there are those who suggest that this should not be done: they argue that the work, together with any accompanying documentation, should be clear and explanatory by itself, so if it needs explaining verbally then there is an inadequacy. If we take this view, then the role of the presenter is merely to say, "yes, I see the bug" or, "yes, I see your point, but the program is OK, it is just the documentation that is misleading, because ...".

Finally, it may enhance the status of walkthroughs if the meeting accepts collective responsibility for the product by deciding that it is satisfactory. Any subsequent problems reflect on the meeting as a whole rather than on the individual programmer. So the meeting is perhaps more likely to be vigilant. If this is done, however, there is a danger of making the walkthrough into something of a trial for an individual who is trying to get his or her work accepted by the group.

After the Walkthrough

Soon after a walkthrough the secretary should distribute copies of the action list decided at the meeting to all the participants. Everyone can then check that the record is correct. The individual programmer whose work was under review will hopefully want to act on the suggestions, possibly after consultation with individual members of the walkthrough team.

If any new errors are detected in the product that has been subjected to a review then it is a good idea to attach responsibility to the whole review team.

12.3 ADVANTAGES AND DISADVANTAGES

Many organizations throughout the world have used structured walkthroughs for some years. Those who report it to be successful endorse the claims of the theoreticians for improvements in:

(a)   software quality
(b)   programmer productivity
(c)   programmer morale
(d)   programmer expertise
(e)   meeting deadlines.

Software Quality

Part of the improved software quality is the dramatically fewer bugs that arise in programs that have been handed over for use by clients. The software is more reliable because bugs have been eliminated by the examination of the program text by a number of people. The program testing may also have been more effective because of the collective construction of test data. In these days when computer systems are increasingly used in on-line applications, some of them life-critical, testing becomes more and more difficult because of the problem of reproducing the real world application. This puts increasing pressure on finding the errors in programs (through some kind of verification or by subjecting them to walkthroughs) before the programs are ever executed.

Another aspect of improved software quality is the ease with which programs can be maintained, that is updated to correct bugs or to accommodate changed user requirements. A program that has been subjected to the scrutiny of a walkthrough is likely to be clearer, more easy to understand. The same is true of the accompanying documentation. Unfortunately, in the past, the first time that the documentation of a program has been studied is long after it has been written. Probably even the author has forgotten all about the program.

Programmer Effort

Most practicing programmers know that the overwhelming proportion of their time is spent in the two activities of clarifying what the program is to do and in debugging the program. The evidence is that structured walkthroughs can greatly reduce the time spent in both of these activities, and therefore programs are completed faster. The time actually spent by all the participants in preparing for and in attending walkthroughs is more than compensated by the saving in programmer's time. It is important to clearly recognize this point, since a common attitude towards walkthroughs is that they waste a good deal of time. Practice has shown that walkthroughs save time. It is found that a week or two's work by one programmer can be reviewed in one session and that by exposing a piece of code to five or six different people, almost all the bugs are eliminated before the program is even run. This avoids the days spent chasing (apparently) obscure bugs using traces, snapshots and other debugging techniques. Suppose that six people spend one hour each in preparation and half an hour at a walkthrough. Then the effort spent is approximately one person-day. A walkthrough might typically deal with 100 lines of COBOL, which at current typical rates for software production takes about 10 person-days to design, code and test. Thus the "overhead" introduced by the walkthrough would be about 10%. Hard evidence is difficult to come by, but the indications are that it is more than justified in terms of savings in the programmer's time.

If, as a programmer, you enjoy spending time debugging them you may not like the idea of walkthroughs. If, on the other hand, you find the design of programs most enjoyable, then walkthroughs may enable you to spend a greater proportion of your time doing just that.

Meeting Deadlines

A recent survey carried out in Britain discovered that the main worry of data processing managers is meeting the deadline for the completion of software. Part of their problem no doubt arises from the fact that managers consistently under-estimate the time required, typically by a factor of two. Management do, of course, commonly apply various forms of pressure on programmers to meet deadlines. But structured walkthroughs can probably help bring the actual time much more into line with estimates, in a much more agreeable way. There are two significant benefits of walkthroughs in this context. First, whereas traditionally major setbacks arise during the testing stage (particularly the integrated system testing), when walkthroughs are used the errors tend to be discovered early, when the cost of correction is low. So catastrophes are rare. Second, because specifications, designs and all aspects of the project are made public in the walkthroughs, there is less chance of something untoward happening without someone noticing. In other words, there can be better project control. This is a thorny issue, as we discuss later, since any management involvement in walkthroughs can seriously damage their success.

Programmer Expertise

Many programmers go through their complete working life without reading a book or an article on programming or without ever discussing techniques with a colleague. No doubt such programmers gain great satisfaction by solving problems on their own. However, structured walkthroughs are a mechanism by which programmers can and do share ideas. Junior programmers in the department can learn from the more experienced, and, perhaps, the other way round. The general level of expertise in the department can be raised.

Programmer Morale

The introduction of structured walkthroughs can contribute to making work more enjoyable in several different ways. First there is the personal satisfaction arising from completing projects more quickly and producing products that are better.

Second, walkthroughs mean that people can find out what other projects are going on in the organization. Programmers can feel more involved in the total work of the department rather than being left out in the cold. Third, learning new techniques from colleagues by looking at their work can be interesting.

Last, but not least, there is the enhanced social aspect to the work; structured walkthroughs switch some of the emphasis of programming from individual contemplation to clear precise communication with others. Part of the satisfaction of going to work arises from meeting people, talking and making friends—walkthroughs extend the opportunities for this activity.

12.4 PROGRAMMERS' WORRIES

There are two major reasons why some programmers are very apprehensive about embarking on a structured walkthrough.

Exposure

One fear is that you might feel as if you had to take your clothes off in public. Since programs are very individual, personal creations you may feel that "reading someone else's program is like reading their private mail—it is an invasion of privacy in which civilized people simply do not indulge".[2] A counter argument to this is that in most organizations nearly every program will eventually be scrutinized by others—the programmers who have to fix the bugs in six months time, or the programmers who have to modify the program to deal with changes in the requirements. The fact is that most programs are studied by several people: the original programmer and the maintenance programmers. This being the case there are two morals:

(a) Our program should be easy to understand in two years time by someone we do not know. (He or she will thank us and respect us for it!)

(b) Expose our feared inadequacies and make a clean breast of it now rather than later. It may well be we have not done anything stupid. If we have, it would be better to find out now, rather than after days of time and trouble.

An alternative suggestion: why don't we show off our work of art to our colleagues rather than to the COBOL compiler? They will appreciate its beauty much more.

It can be really exciting to examine someone else's program and find out how they think, or to discover a new technique. On the other hand we cannot expect to look at someone else's programs without letting them look at ours. It can be gratifying to find some errors in our colleague's program, thus saving him or her hours of frustration. Conversely, our colleagues can save us a lot of time.

The point is that everyone makes mistakes. Even one of today's programming gurus is attributed with saying, "We are all human". Presumably he implies that even he makes errors when writing programs. If we recognize this, and realize that errors can be more quickly resolved by collective means, then programming can become a much more sociable and enjoyable activity.

Programmer Appraisal

The second worry that many programmers have, has a much more serious and sinister basis. It concerns assessment, pay and promotion.

A programmer may well feel that if his or her work is subjected to a walkthrough then the project leader or manager will be able to assess much more clearly the quality of the work and how long it takes the programmer to do it. He or she sees that this may well affect a pay rise or promotion chances.

In many organizations a programmer perceives (correctly) that there are only a limited number of senior positions and that he or she is in competition with the other programmers for them. This competitive arena is fostered by some managements in the hope of getting people to work harder. Even if all the programmers in your organization were brilliant, there is no way that your management would pay you all the same high salary.

There is no doubt that if management are involved in structured walkthroughs then they have much greater insight into and control over what is going on. So the question is whether management are going to be able to appraise you more fairly with or without information gained from structured walkthroughs. This raises the issue of how a manager judges a programmer in the absence of walkthroughs.

While some organizations formalize their appraisal procedures, in others the programmers are left to believe that it may well be their timekeeping or manner of dress that determines their pay as much as their adherence to project deadlines. Even where attention is paid to programmer productivity there must be great doubts about the validity of the process. The evidence is so overwhelming that it is nearly impossible to estimate the length of time that it should or will take to develop a piece of software, so the judgement of a programmer on the basis of the estimated time to complete a program is highly suspect.

If you like the idea of walkthrough but you are concerned that management's involvement would inhibit free discussion and therefore sabotage the very idea of walkthroughs then try to persuade management not to take part in or be involved in any way in the walkthroughs. After all, the essential benefit of a walkthrough will be achieved without management involvement. Many managers appreciate this anyway. They therefore stay away from walkthroughs and do not look at the minutes.

We do not claim that there is any easy answer to this problem of using the information from walkthroughs as a basis for programmer assessment. Indeed, it is probably the most difficult issue. Perhaps the discussion of the problem with your own colleagues in the light of your own circumstances can help your organization arrive at a satisfactory way of doing things.

12.5 DESIGN AND CODE INSPECTIONS

A technique which bears a superficial similarity to structured walkthroughs is called inspections. These inspections normally take place at two points during program development—after the design is complete and after the coding is complete (hence the titles).

Inspections are similar to structured walkthroughs in that a group of people meet to review a piece of work, but they are different from walkthroughs in several respects. Checklists are used to ensure that no relevant considerations are ignored. Errors that are discovered are classified according to type and meticulously recorded on forms. Statistics on errors are computed, for example in terms of errors per 1 000 lines of code. Thus, inspections are not just well organized, they are completely formal. In addition management is informed of the results of inspections, though usually they do not attend the meeting.

There are other, minor, differences between inspections and walkthroughs. Normally there are only four members in an inspection team: the *moderator*, who coordinates activities; the *designer* who designed the program component being inspected; the *implementor*—the programmer who will program the component (in a design inspection) or who has programmed the component (in a code inspection); and the *tester*—a person who acts as someone who will be responsible for testing the component.

The essence of inspections is that the study of designs and programs is carried out under close management supervision. Thus, inspections are overtly a mechanism for increased control over programmers' work, in a similar fashion to the way that quality control is carried out on a factory floor. Many programmers would feel threatened in this situation and become defensive, perhaps trying to hide their mistakes. It is not clear how such a situation can improve the discovery of errors, let alone make programming a more enjoyable activity.

IBM have actively tried to publicize inspections. They claim that inspections give even greater programmer productivity and fewer errors than structured walkthroughs.

12.6 SUMMARY

Structured walkthroughs are based on the premise that ideas that are shared will be the better for it. Organizations that have successfully used the technique report (in some cases) dramatic improvements in software quality and in the time taken to produce it.

The careful organization of a walkthrough is important. The most important points are:

(a) the time taken for a walkthrough should be restricted (say to half an hour)

(b)   participants must receive and study the material prior to the meeting
(c)   the chairperson must be in control.

Programmers are often apprehensive about walkthroughs because their inadequacies will be exposed to the public gaze. For this reason it is vital that:

(a)   management do not attend the meetings
(b)   participants at the meeting concentrate on the program, *not* on the programmer.

When they are successful, structured walkthroughs can contribute to a friendly team spirit and thereby a more enjoyable working environment.

Some organizations have transformed the idea of walkthroughs into a much more formal technique known as inspections. These probably give greater management control, but may well cause programmers to feel increasingly under scrutiny.

12.7 REFERENCES AND FURTHER READING

1.   Weinberg, G. M., *The Psychology of Computer Programming*, Van Nostrand Reinhold, New York, 1971.
      This is the book in which the idea of ego-less programming, the forerunner of structured walkthroughs, was suggested.

2.   Yourdon, E., "Making the Move to Structured Programming", *Datamation*, June 1975, pp. 52–56.

3.   Yourdon, E., *Structured Walkthroughs* (2nd. ed.), Prentice-Hall, Englewood Cliffs, N.J., 1979.
      We feel this book tends to underplay the programmer's view of life. There is a lot of disucssion of the psychology of interactions within groups.

12.8 EXERCISES

1.   Do you think structured walkthroughs would be effective in your organization? Why? If they would be effective, how could they be introduced?

2.   Try to introduce ego-less programming into your organization in the following way. When you have written your next program and have a clean-compiled listing, ask one of your colleagues to look through it for you. Explain that you would appreciate comments of any kind on the program's clarity, correctness, etc. Explain that you are trying to identify problems sooner rather than later. Offer to do the same in return.

13

Chief Programmer Teams and Project Support Libraries

13.1 INTRODUCTION

This chapter is about organizational structure that is imposed on a team of programmers by management. It is not about the informal social processes that go on within a group of people who work together. If your interest is in such things as power struggles, leadership and democracy in a team we give some suggested reading at the end of the chapter. The concern of this chapter is with methods of controlling the work of a team of programmers engaged on constructing parts of the same large piece of software.

We begin by analyzing some of the problems of group work. We go on to explain two important techniques for team organization—the program production library and the chief programmer team. We conclude by discussing the pros and cons of these techniques as they may be perceived by both the programmers in the team and the management of the organization.

Two major aspects of team activity are:

(a) the communication between the people in the team
(b) deciding who does what work.

We discuss these issues in turn.

When two or more people are working on a piece of software they obviously have to liaise with each other. At the very least they have to communicate module specifications—module names, module functions, parameter types and so on. Often such interfaces are complex, perhaps

205

involving detailed file layouts. Always there are queries, because of the difficulty of precisely specifying interfaces. During the lifetime of a project someone always leaves, or is ill, or goes on holiday. Someone has to sort out the work in their absence. New people join the team and have to understand what the software is for, what has been done and why the structure is as it is. They may need to learn about the standards and procedures being used on the project, or even learn a new programming language. This induction of a new person takes up the time of the other members of the team.

All this adds up to a great deal of time spent in communication that would not be necessary if a single person only were developing the software. Adding two people to a team of four does not increase the communication overhead by half—it more than doubles it. Clearly, as more and more people are added to a team the time taken in liaising can completely swamp a project. To make matters worse, human beings are not well-known for precise communication with each other. Thus it is likely that there will be faults in a system constructed by a team.

We have assumed in all of this that each and every team member communicates with every other. We shall see that this is what the Chief Programmer Team organization attempts to avoid.

The second major question in team organization is deciding how to break down the complete task of constructing a large piece of software into smaller tasks so that several people can carry them out. This is not purely the technical issue of how to decompose a system into suitable modules; there are other ways of splitting up the work. Any programmer knows that he or she spends only about 10% of his time actually programming (by which we mean coding). The rest of the time is spent in activities like program design, testing and writing documentation. Programmers carry out a whole variety of tasks, some of which, like design, are challenging and others, like keying corrections or filing listings are less demanding. One way of dividing the work of software development amongst a set of people is to separate out tasks requiring different degrees of skill so that for example, one person does all the design and another all the keypunching.

This principle of the division of labor has long been recognized. A major feature of this type of organization is that instead of paying several highly skilled people good wages, management can pay people who have different skills different salaries. Overall the wages of the people with unequal skills will be lower than those of the skilled people, thus the wages bill is reduced. To give a crude example, it would be cheaper to employ a programmer at $10 000 and an analyst at $20 000, rather than to employ two analyst/programmers each at $17 000.

It is no coincidence that Charles Babbage, one of the founding fathers of computing, was well aware of this effect. As long ago as 1832, in his book *On the Economy of Machine and Manufacturers*, Babbage wrote:[1]

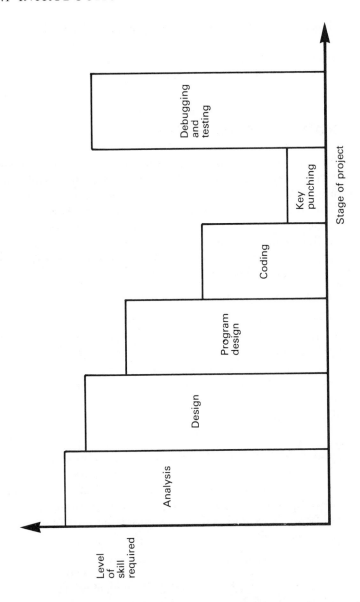

Fig. 13.1 Skill requirements at various stages of a project.

The master manufacturer, by dividing the work to be executed into different processes, each requiring different degrees of skill or of force, can purchase exactly that precise quality of both which is necessary for each process; whereas, if the whole work were executed by one workman, that person must possess sufficient skill to perform the most difficult, and sufficient strength to execute the most laborious, of the operations into which the art is divided.

Figure 13.1 illustrates a possible view of the changing skills involved during the developments of software.

Both program production libraries and Chief Programmer Teams exploit this principle of the division of labor.

13.2 PROGRAM PRODUCTION LIBRARY

The technique of using a program production library is also known as project support library, program development library and development support library. Essentially the idea is to take away from each of the programmers in a team the least skilled parts of their work. This tends to be the work of a clerical nature. These tasks are assigned to a single person known as the librarian. The idea is to enhance the productivity of the programmers by allowing them to spend more of their time doing what they are good at, namely programming.

The librarian carries out the following work:

(a)   accepts requests (usually in writing) from programmers
(b)   updates source code from listings that are marked up
(c)   carries out key-punching
(d)   submits computer runs—compilations or testing
(e)   maintains files of documents relating to the project both in a human readable form and in a machine readable form
(f)   maintains back-up copies of all files and restores them where necessary.

The programmers in the team never use the computer themselves. Whenever they want anything done on the computer they ask the librarian to do it. Another significant change to the programmers' lifestyle is that all documents associated with the project, including current listings, are maintained by the librarian. This implies that the status of the work of the project is much more visible to all concerned.

The librarian looks after two libraries:

(a)   the internal library, inside the computer, that contains all current project information, e.g.:
    (i)   source code
    (ii)   object code
    (iii) link edit commands
    (iv)   store image code
    (v)   job control statements
    (vi)   test data

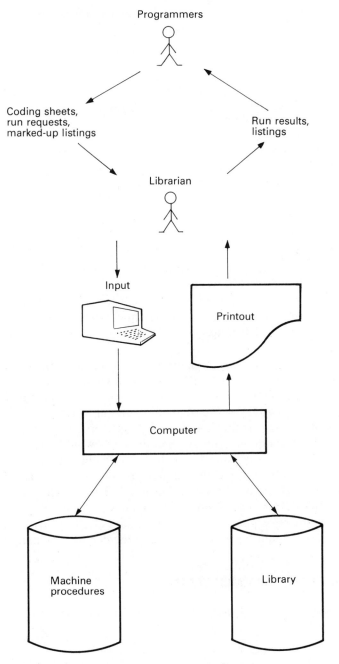

Fig. 13.2 People and computer in the project support library.

(b)   the external library, which is human readable and contains current and archived copies of the information in the internal library.

The librarian works according to two sets of procedures:

(a)   machine procedure for carrying out operations on the internal library, e.g.:
    (i)   updating files
    (ii)   performing compilations
    (iii)   link editing
    (iv)   running tests
    (v)   obtaining listings
    (vi)   backing-up and restoring files
(b)   office procedures, for the clerical aspects of the project, e.g.:
    (i)   filing
    (ii)   status reports
    (iii)   receiving instructions from the programmers.

The relationships between the programmer, the librarian and the computer may be described as shown in Fig. 13.2.

The fact that the programmers in the team are relieved of some of their tasks has another effect. Because the programmers are doing more, fewer of them are required, which in turn means that less time is wasted in communication.

Note also that the programmers need not concern themselves with writing job control language, which is commonly a major source of errors and time wasting. Only one person, the librarian, is concerned with job control language, and he or she becomes expert at it. Hence, the librarian does not make the errors that a number of programmers (concerned essentially with the programming rather than the j.c.l.) would make.

With the trend away from the batch development of programs towards interactive development facilities and increasingly sophisticated workbenches, it is not clear how the separation of tasks between the programmers and the librarian can be organized, or whether it is still desirable. In a sense, a good programming support environment automatically provides many of the services that could formerly have been provided by a human librarian.

13.3 CHIEF PROGRAMMER TEAM

The general ideas behind the Chief Programmer Team organization are:

(a)   to divide the work amongst skilled specialists
(b)   to structure the team in a well-defined way so that each individual's role is clear, and communication is minimized.

Comparison is made with a surgical team in which the chief surgeon is assisted by an assistant surgeon, an anesthetist, and one or two nurses. In the Chief Programmer Team the job titles are Chief Programmer, Back-up Programmer, Librarian and other programmers as and when necessary.

Other techniques already described in this book are usually employed in conjunction with the team organization. They are the program production library, top-down implementation and testing, and functional decomposition.

The roles of the team members are:

Chief Programmer. This is a highly skilled programmer who produces the high-level parts of the system such as the job control language statements and link edit commands. If there is some crucial controlling part to the system, like the nucleus of the operating system, he or she does this as well.

The Chief Programmer specifies all the other components in the system and oversees the integration or system testing of the complete system. The Chief Programmer's role is intended to be almost entirely a technical one. To this end administrative affairs like reporting to management and monitoring budgets are dealt with by a Project Manager. The Project Manager is not really part of the team and usually will deal with the administrative aspects of several teams.

Back-up Programmer. This is a programmer whose skill is comparable to that of the Chief Programmer. The job is to help the Chief Programmer with his or her tasks and act as the Chief Programmer when the latter is absent through illness or holidays. Should the Chief Programmer leave the organization the back-up programmer can immediately take over.

Librarian. The librarian maintains the program production library as described above. He or she is usually a secretary with some training in keypunching and submitting computer runs. A secretary is often used to following a well-defined set of procedures and is good at typing and maintaining files.

Other programmers. When needed, other programmers are brought into the team to develop subsystems specified by the Chief Programmer. Each of these programmers is probably expert in a particular software area like filing systems or mathematical subroutines.

The structure of the team is hierarchical, with the Chief Programmer at the top. In contrast to a network of people each of whom communicates with everyone else, the hierarchy restricts information so that it flows along far fewer paths—only up and down the hierarchy. The use of structured programming and top-down implementation and testing, both of which are hierarchical, fit in with this scheme very neatly.

13.4 ADVANTAGES AND DISADVANTAGES

There can be no doubt that the techniques of the program production library and the Chief Programmer Team represent a creative application of scientific management to team programming. It can be no surprise to learn that the techniques were conceived and first implemented by IBM. Whether the techniques are good or bad depends on your value system. Certainly IBM are continuing to use them and claim that they are effective. On the other hand some see the techniques as eroding programmers' skills and making the work more routine.

From the management point of view the division of labor gives:

(a) control over the work process by management
(b) greater productivity, since the team member does just one type of work; he or she, therefore, becomes very good at it
(c) the possibility of automating some aspects of the work
(d) the chance to pay the different team members according to the separate skills involved in their work, rather than pay everyone at the same rate for the highly-skilled work.

The benefits of these two team methods to the organization are thus:

(a) improved programmer productivity because
   (i) programmers are freed from clerical tasks
   (ii) there are clearer interfaces between programmers through use of the library
   (iii) less time is spent in communication because there are fewer programmers in the team
(b) improved software quality because
   (i) the team is organized around a highly skilled programmer
   (ii) the interfaces between software components are clearer
   (iii) there are fewer bugs arising from communication problems because there are fewer programmers
   (iv) the use of the well maintained library encourages modularity
(c) meeting deadlines reliably because
   (i) there is greater visibility of the project through the high technical involvement of the Chief Programmer and the use of the library
   (ii) using the program production library enforces disciplined working

Other benefits that are cited concern career paths. First, someone who is a good programmer but does not want to go into management, can become a Chief Programmer—largely a technical role. Second, it is said that the job of librarian may be attractive to a secretary, because it involves computer-related tasks. It is not considered a suitable job for a junior programmer who would probably be dissatisfied with the many clerical aspects of the work.

A number of problems arise for management. First, since any team is only manageable with up to about nine people, what do you do if a project is sufficiently large that it needs more than this number? One suggestion (but it is only that) is to start the project with a Chief Programmer Team to carry out the high level software design and the top-level implementation. When this is complete the original team is broken up and its members become Chief Programmers within the set of teams that carry out developments of the subsystems. A remnant of the original team carries out system integration and validation.

Another problem of Chief Programmer Team organization, is that since the team is supposed to be made up of good experienced programmers, how do inexperienced programmers gain expertise? Here the suggestion is that they should cut their teeth on maintenance of existing programs.

Although everyone likes to work for a successful organization, the goals of the management and the programmers do not always coincide. Essentially the management is concerned with profitability, and it is therefore in its interests to try to gain greater control over programming and to de-skill the job as far as possible. On the other hand many programmers are interested in a good salary, interesting or even stimulating work, variety, learning more sophisticated skills and remaining free of undue management surveillance.

The team techniques we have described tend to remove variety from the job (even doing some keypunching makes a change now and again). By the same token, programmers spend longer on the demanding aspects of programming, which means they may be more tired at the end of the day. The use of a program production library means that they can no longer work in the way they like best—they are constrained by the established procedures. Finally, the increased visibility of the work, always on view in the library, can induce stress.

13.5 SUMMARY

There are two major problems with organizing a team that has been set-up to develop a piece of software. One is preventing the overhead of communication between team members from overwhelming the project. The other is deciding how the work should be divided amongst the members of the team.

The idea of the program production library is to strip from the programmers the clerical aspect of their work—keypunching, filing and so on. This makes them more productive in their prime function, programming. It also reduces the number of programmers necessary in the team, thus reducing the communication problem. Last, but not least, all the documentation on the project is well-organized and easily viewed.

The idea of the Chief Programmer Team is to use a few, specialized people each performing a well defined task within a hierarchical organization with minimal communication paths. Thus, the number of people in the team is reduced and the communication overhead controlled.

Both techniques mean that the programming task is brought under greater management control and visibility, which probably leads to greater productivity, an improved ability to meet deadlines, and enhanced software quality. Certainly IBM, who use these techniques extensively, report enormous gains in these areas.

From the individual programmer's point of view, though it can be satisfying to work in a well organized and successful team, it may be that the increased control over his or her work and work methods brings dissatisfaction. There is evidence to support this latter view.

13.6 REFERENCES AND FURTHER READING

1. Babbage, C., *On the Economy of Machine and Manufacturers.*

2. Weinberg, G .M., *The Psychology of Computer Programming*, Van Nostrand Reinhold, New York, 1971.
    This classic book deals at length and in a most interesting way with the informal, social aspects of working in a team.

3. Kraft, P., *Programmers and Managers*, Springer Verlag, New York, 1977.
    This book analyses the software development process in our society, comparing it with other types of work. While you may not agree with the analysis, you must be prepared to argue with it.

13.7 EXERCISES

1. Investigate the importance of the time taken in communicating within a team. Assume initially that there are four people in a team. Each is capable of developing 3 000 lines of code, per year, left to themselves. However, 250 lines per year are sacrificed for each communication path to or from an individual. Assume that the team is organized so that everyone needs to discuss problems with everyone else.
    Calculate the productivity (lines of code per year) of each member of the team and investigate how it changes as the team expands to six and then to eight members.

2. Carry out the same calculations assuming that a Chief Programmer Team is in operation. (In this case each member of the team communicates only with the Chief Programmer.)

3. Estimate how much of a programmer's time would be saved if he or she did not have to carry out the clerical parts of the job because a program production library was available.

INDEX

215